# A GUIDE

## ～ *to* ～

# MISSISSIPPI
# MUSEUMS

### DIANE WILLIAMS
### AND RICHELLE PUTNAM

*Foreword by Malcolm White*

THE
History
PRESS

Published by The History Press
Charleston, SC
www.historypress.com

Copyright © 2024 by Diane Williams and Richelle Putnam
All rights reserved

*Front cover, clockwise from top left*: courtesy of Richelle Putnam; courtesy of Mary Beth Agee; courtesy of Richelle Putnam; courtesy of Richelle Putnam; courtesy of Richelle Putnam.
*Back cover, left*: courtesy of Delta Blues Museum; *top right*: courtesy of Diane Williams; *bottom right*: courtesy of Sondra Lee Bell.

First published 2024

Manufactured in the United States

ISBN 9781467141840

Library of Congress Control Number: 9781467141840

*Notice*: The information in this book is true and complete to the best of our knowledge. It is offered without guarantee on the part of the authors or The History Press. The authors and The History Press disclaim all liability in connection with the use of this book.

*To my devoted husband, who supports my writing life; my children, who still enjoy exploring museums; and my grandchildren, who already love discovering people and places of the past.*
*—Richelle*

*To James and Jackson, my grandson-shines; and to Perry and Tim, the parents who are raising them to enjoy museums.*
*—Diane*

# CONTENTS

# FOREWORD

Telling the Mississippi story is what our museums do—hold memories and stories, Mississippi's most valuable asset. As physical places, museums boldly narrate the tales of the past by uncovering the courage, determination, persistence and commitment of those before us and preserve their experiences through collections and exhibits. In these varied histories of diverse cultures lie the personal accounts of our artists, innovators, leaders, advocates and their work—our Mississippi humanities. We are a people of storytellers, and our stories and trail markers lead us and visitors alike in amazement and delight around the state.

We have not always gotten things right, but in the arena of arts and culture and story, we wrote the book. And our cultural centers and institutions of story (museums) play a major part in that success. Where history is made, when art erupts, we mark it, we erect a creative signpost and call it a trail, and our trails lead to our museums and collectively create economic and community development and, more importantly, instill civic pride. These temples of intangibles, this "sense of place" that Miss Welty reminds us is our birthright, are our best offering of who we are, what happened and where.

Often last on the list we want to be first on and first on the list we wish to be last on, we remain unrivaled and unparalleled on the list of who's who in art, history and culture. We made this mark, this X on the map that says visit, learn and be amazed.

I am delighted that these dear friends, these two powerful, creative women, have collaborated here to tell the story of the remarkable museums of Mississippi.

—Malcolm White
Former director,
Visit Mississippi and Mississippi Arts Commission

8

# INTRODUCTION

As Mississippi heralds a callout from every corner, shouting, "Look at me!" we are reminded of Tennessee Williams's opening essay, "Person to Person," for *Cat on a Hot Tin Roof*. Williams's anecdote describes a young girl and her friends, all dressed up, all trying to gain the others' attention on a street in Mississippi. A young girl falls into the mud and shouts, "Look at me! Look at me!"

This book heralds a call to "look at communities," large and small around the state, that developed a deeper understanding of Mississippi's past and the need to move forward and be accountable to its truths with accurate accounts. In turn, these communities formed historical societies, genealogy groups and archival and research centers to learn broader perspectives of their history. Today, over 220 museums, historic homes and culture centers around the state showcase regional, state and worldwide stories, bringing them to life through archives, exhibitions, live events, films, presentations and programs.

Mississippi's history embodies each region's culture, industry, military, agriculture, landscape, waterscape, wildlife, festivals, arts, crafts, folklife, folklore, myths and diverse population. Often referred to as the "Birthplace of America's Music," Mississippi boasts so many country and blues music markers that, if they could talk, would say, "We're not stopping here!" Museums around the state highlight legendary musicians who were either born or lived in the region and whose genius initiated specific sounds that evolved into various genres. Three world-renowned notables are Meridian's

Jimmie Rodgers (the "Father of Country Music"), Indianola's B.B. King (the "King of the Blues") and Tupelo's Elvis Presley (the "King of Rock 'n' Roll"). Other communities recognize their household-name musicians, like Bo Diddley and Vasti Jackson (McComb), Robert Johnson (Greenwood, Crystal Springs and Hazelhurst), Marty Stuart (Philadelphia) and Howlin' Wolf (West Point).

Mississippi's distinct landscapes are typically divided into four geographic regions: Pine Belt (Piney Woods or Southern Pine Hills), Northern Hills, Gulf Coast and Yazoo Basin (the Delta). Within these regions are more distinguishing landforms, like the Northern or Red Clay Hills, Flatwoods, Pontotoc Ridge, the Tishomingo or Northeastern Hills, the Black Prairie, the strip of limestone soil that stretches from Alabama and the Loess Plateau or Loess Bluff region formed during the Ice Age. These different landforms drew distinctly different cultures to settle in each. The first inhabitants were the Native Americans, who settled their villages, built their sacred mounds and hunted and fished the land and waters until the infringement of early European explorers. Across the state, museums reveal their region's Native American history, like Desoto County Museum, Jaketown Museum, Winterville Mounds and Museum and, more specifically, Chahta Immi Cultural Center.

Settlers from the eastern and northern parts of the country and immigrants from other countries chose various regions in Mississippi to meet their entrepreneurial goals and family needs. Those dealing in cotton, from growing to warehousing, often chose the Delta and agricultural areas capable of producing high yields of cotton. Those histories are now at the public's disposal through museums like the Aaron Cotton Company Museum in Clarksdale, the Century of History Museum in Greenville, the Museum of the Mississippi Delta in Greenwood and the Magnolia Hall in Natchez.

In the American South, "King Cotton" and the enslaved labor required to plant, tend and harvest the crop became the catalyst for the American Civil War, probably the most covered topic in the museums of Mississippi. Various perspectives of the war's effect on the communities, families, soldiers and formerly enslaved can be found at the Greenwood Blues Heritage Museum and Gallery, the Marshall County Historical Museum in Holly Springs, Brice's Cross Roads National Battlefield and Corinth Civil War Interpretive Center.

Northern timber magnates who deforested most of the South chose Mississippi's pine woods region, where cutting timber, sawmilling and turpentining became lucrative professions. Peter Little of Natchez and the

Laurel Eastman Rogers family of Laurel are highlighted in the Rosalie Mansion and Gardens and the Lauren Rogers Museum, respectively. That lumber industry is proficiently illustrated through the Mississippi Industrial Heritage Museum, which resides in the factory building that manufactured lumber products from 1885 until the 1930s, when the industry depleted the state's pine forests. Most cutover land was not suitable for farming, which caused greater environmental and economic havoc during the Great Depression. Other museums reveal how communities confronted this devastating financial downturn period, like Corinth's Borroum's Drug Store and Soda Fountain, which created the affordable slug burger, and Meridian's Al and Fred Key, who set a world-record endurance flight during the Depression. (For more on this topic, see *Mississippi and the Great Depression* by Richelle Putnam.)

At the NASA John C. Stennis Space Center and INFINITY Science Center in Pearlington, science, aeronautics and aerospace are illuminated. Plants and insects are highlighted at the Mississippi Entomological Museum in Starkville. Several Mississippi Gulf Coast locations, like the Maritime & Seafood Industry Museum, Marine Education Center and Institute for Marine Mammal Studies, display maritime history and research. These outstanding Mississippi observatories open their doors to visitors from all over the world.

Waterways have an incredible history, and museums north, south, east and west inform visitors how the Mississippi River and other waterways positively and negatively contributed to communities economically, socially and travel-wise. The 1927 Flood Museum, River Road Queen Welcome Center and Museum of the Delta, Tunica RiverPark Museum, Jesse Brent Lower Mississippi River Museum and Catfish Row Museum all share different stories from different eras through various perspectives.

During the late 1800s, Mississippi's primary industries were timber and railroad construction. Railroads provided transportation of goods, such as cotton and wood, and of people. They, therefore, became the primary economic engine for regions like the Delta, the Piney Woods, the river cities and the Gulf Coast. Martin and Sue King Railroad Heritage Museum, Casey Jones Railroad Museum, Crossroads Museum and the Historic Corinth Depot and Sam Wilhite Transportation Museum are some venues overseeing this history.

Also connected to the railroads is Mississippi's civil rights history. Although the Civil War ended slavery, Mississippi politicians claimed the authority to regulate race relations. After Reconstruction ended in 1877, they devised methods to establish racial segregation and suppress the majority Black population. In 1888, the Mississippi legislature directed railroads to "provide equal but separate accommodations for the white and colored races by providing two or more passenger cars for each passenger train." The Mississippi Supreme Court decision upheld this law. Mississippi civil rights activist Ida B. Wells challenged the laws denying her access to the white ladies' car. Her life is celebrated in the Ida B. Wells Barnett Museum in Holly Springs. Although the U.S. Supreme Court upheld the power of the state legislatures for decades, the 1950s and 1960s civil rights movement continued to challenge that decision. This fight for equality in Mississippi continued with the Reverend George Lee, "Father of the Voter Registration Movement," and Fannie Lou Hamer, both honored in Belzoni museums. Other museums, specifically the Civil Rights Museum and Smith Robertson Museum and Cultural Center in Jackson, celebrate Mississippi African Americans who hurdled over the obstacles and roadblocks of Jim Crow laws to become successful entrepreneurs, politicians, social activists, writers, performers and film and radio personalities.

Religion in Mississippi is as diverse as its topography and has played an enormous role not only in providing the space for museums but also in establishing the institutions where many museums are located, like Rust College, the location of the Roy Wilkins Collection at the Leontyne Price Library, and the Yellow Fever Martyrs Church & Museum, both in Holly Springs. The Yellow Fever Martyrs Museum is a testament to the martyrs who, with limited understanding of how to treat dying individuals during an epidemic, struggled to save a city ravaged by the disease before the discovery of vaccinations. Some historic church buildings house museums, like the Burns-Belfry Museum & Multicultural Center in Oxford, and some churches were important enough to move to a museum site, like Elvis Presley's childhood church, the Assembly of God Pentecostal Church in Tupelo. Visitors gain better insight and understanding of religions outside the Christian faith, such as the Muslim faith highlighted at the International Museum of Muslim Cultures and the Jewish faith portrayed at the Museum of Jewish Experience.

Mississippi produced some of the world's greatest literary giants: William Faulkner, Eudora Welty, Richard Wright, Tennessee Williams and John Grisham. Their lives and literary works will always be remembered through centers like the Mississippi Arts and Entertainment Experience, Rowan Oak, the Eudora Welty House, Smith Robertson Museum and Cultural Center, the Tennessee Williams House & Welcome Center Museum and the John

Grisham Room at Mississippi State University. But there are other museum surprises to be seen, including an Armitage carousel from the turn of the twentieth century, a museum celebrating the game of bridge, a clock museum, Coca-Cola museums, a GRAMMY museum and the Mississippi State Hospital, once known as an insane asylum, which preserves and documents early treatments of mental illness at their museum in Whitfield. No topic goes uncovered, from the ordinary people who accomplished extraordinary things to film stars, singers, musicians, military officials, governors and even presidents. In fact, there is a museum celebrating the lives of U.S. presidents Abraham Lincoln and Ulysses S. Grant.

This book became a four-year endeavor due to the COVID-19 pandemic, which halted our visitation efforts for three years. As we researched the plethora of museums, we received enormous satisfaction knowing that many survived the pandemic. In the interim, we learned that some did not. Tupelo's Automobile Museum opened in 2002 and auctioned off 174 of the finest collection of cars after showcasing its vehicles for almost twenty years. Still, we remain encouraged to see new museums opening around the state and welcome Mound Bayou's Museum of African American Culture and

Tupelo Automobile Museum (closed). *Courtesy of Sondra Lee Bell.*

Tupelo Automobile Museum (closed). *Courtesy of Sondra Lee Bell.*

Tupelo Automobile Museum (closed). *Courtesy of Sondra Lee Bell.*

History, Marty Stuart's Congress of Country Music and the newly renovated Ellis Theater in downtown Philadelphia.

Mississippians perpetuate the desire to preserve who they are, and more museums will rise in their communities. We commit to sharing and updating museum news with tourists and history buffs through the upcoming Mississippi Museums website. *A Guide to Mississippi Museums* is the reader's ticket to explore, research, learn, interact with and celebrate what a genuinely majestic state, in all its glory and with all its bruises, is all about.

Part I

# THE DELTA

Aaron Cotton Company Museum
311 Delta Avenue
Clarksdale, MS 38614

William Edgar Aaron founded the Aaron Cotton Company in the "Golden Buckle of the Cotton Belt" (Clarksdale) in 1950. The museum highlights old farming tools, appliances and equipment used for cotton farming and mimics what the old cotton office looked like years ago. All things cotton is the mantra here, including opportunities for visitors to purchase cotton and cotton seeds and learn about the history of the blues. The Aaron Cotton Company Museum is the perfect place to visit during the Juke Joint Blues Festival in April. The festival celebrates the blues and brags about its "monkeys riding dogs and pig races."

American Contract Bridge League Museum and
   Bridge Hall of Fame
6575 Windchase Boulevard
Horn Lake, MS 38637

The American Contract Bridge League Museum celebrates the history of the game of bridge. Founded in 1937, the American Contract Bridge League made its home in Horn Lake in 2010, boasting over 165,000 members. A trip to the museum enlightens visitors with photos, art, national championship trophies "that must be seen to be believed," videos, instructional material and interactive technology recognizing names and championships from around the world. Inside the museum are the Albert H. Morehead Memorial Library and the Bridge Hall of Fame, which *Bridge World* magazine started in 1964. The Joan Schepps Collection of Trump Indicators includes six hundred colorful pieces, the Blackwood Award and the von Zedtwitz Awardees (showcasing past winners).

American Heritage "Big Red" Fire Museum
332 North Church Avenue
Louisville, MS 39339

The American Heritage "Big Red" Fire Museum in downtown Louisville stores an antique fire truck and a vintage firefighting equipment collection. There is also a man-drawn and horse-drawn fire apparatus equipped with a water tower that carried water to the flames, as well as a 1797 hand pumper once used in Plymouth, Massachusetts, with leather hose and a bucket brigade system pulled and operated by manpower. Managed by Lex Taylor, the museum was made possible by Lex's father, Bill Taylor, who longed to educate and provide research for curiosity seekers. The museum periodically hosts education programs and other events.

B.B. King Museum and Delta Interpretive Center
200 Second Street
Indianola, MS 38751

The mission of the B.B. King Museum and Delta Interpretive Center is to "empower, unite, and heal through music, art and education and to share the Mississippi Delta's rich cultural heritage." The unified effort highlights the blues and the greatest bluesman in the industry. The B.B. King Museum takes visitors on an interactive journey, from hands-on, interpretive media to education and performances. Memorabilia and artifacts, like King's personal papers, news items and objects from his life and work, along with innovative multimedia and film, reflect on the life of the legendary musician and provide information about the music industry. Visitors watch videos on King's life and live performances in the theater. Adjoining the museum is a large, open, airy room that was once the old gin where Riley "B.B." King

B.B. King Museum and Delta Interpretive Center. *Courtesy of Rory Doyle & B.B. King Museum.*

worked as a young man. The museum exhibits are based on five themes: (1) the land and place, (2) blues history and the music's relationship to African American history, (3) the character of the music to the people, (4) interracial diversity and (5) how these things impacted the music of B.B. King. Tony Mendez created the outside bronze sculpture of King overlooking the museum. The Lucille Museum Gift Shop is named after King's guitar.

CARNEGIE PUBLIC LIBRARY ARCHEOLOGY COLLECTION
114 DELTA AVENUE
CLARKSDALE, MS 38614

Named after Andrew Carnegie, a businessman and philanthropist who was instrumental in building libraries around the world, this facility in Clarksdale is a place where the community can come for a multitude of library services. The Carnegie Public Library has something that most libraries do not have. Its displays of Mississippi pottery, artifacts and archaeological research materials provide a sense of place to residents in Clarksdale and Coahoma County. These artifacts are uniquely displayed and curated in a room where visitors can enjoy them.

CATFISH MUSEUM AND WELCOME CENTER
111 MAGNOLIA STREET
BELZONI, MS 39038

Former governor Cliff Finch deemed Humphreys County the "Catfish Capital" of the world because of its U.S. farm-raised catfish industry. Situated in the IB&B Depot in downtown Belzoni, the Catfish Museum and Welcome Center celebrates the history and culture of Humphreys County. Welcoming visitors out front is the "King Cat," the world's largest catfish sculpture, measuring forty feet in height. Other sculptures include mixed-media designs made of spawning cans, hatchery tanks and fishing nets. The museum boasts the most extensive collection of outdoor sculptures in any location in the state. Inside the museum is a celebration of handiworks by members of the Craftsmen's Guild of Mississippi. Around the town of Belzoni are various artistic catfish sculptures. In April, the town of Belzoni hosts a World Catfish Festival.

CENTURY OF HISTORY MUSEUM AT THE HEBREW UNION TEMPLE
504 MAIN STREET
GREENVILLE, MS 38701

Located in a nineteenth-century Reform synagogue, the Century of History Museum teaches and informs the public about the Jewish community's impact from the 1800s to the present in the Mississippi Delta and Greenville, once home to Mississippi's largest Jewish population, including the Greenville Steins, who were the founders of Stein Mart Department Store. Exhibits include a Torah recovered after World War I, a history of Adolf Hitler, information on Greenville's first mayor and items related to the military. Along with displays, a Photo Memory Wall reflects the social life of early settlers, cobblers, bankers, merchants, plantation owners, cotton traders, factory owners, farmers from Germanic countries, Russian Jewish settlers and more. The museum documents those early days, when the area persevered through hardship, such as the Great Fire of 1874, the Yellow Fever in 1878 and the Great Flood of 1927.

CHARLES W. CAPPS ARCHIVES AND MUSEUM
DELTA STATE UNIVERSITY
101 FIFTH AVENUE
CLEVELAND, MS 38733

Delta State University's Charles W. Capps Archives and Museum is a three-story structure named in honor of Charles Wilson "Charlie" Capps Jr., a former Mississippi state representative. The museum houses a gallery and reception/seminar room. It serves as a depository for historical, political, social and geographical documents and artifacts vital to the Delta area and Mississippi. Collections include oral histories documenting German POWs incarcerated in the Mississippi Delta during World War II (1942–45), Chinese families living in the Mississippi Delta, African American farmers and civil rights participants. There are over four hundred oral history interviews covering a wide range of subjects concerning the history and culture of the Mississippi Delta. The Mississippi Delta Chinese Museum is located on the third floor. The facility also houses a baseball museum, the Robert L. Crawford Center, which opened in 2007.

DELTA BLUES MUSEUM
1 BLUES ALLEY
CLARKSDALE, MS 38614

The Delta Blues Museum considers itself a storyteller of the blues. Established in 1979 by the Carnegie Public Library Board of Trustees and Sid Graves, the museum's first location was an elementary school. In 1981, the museum moved to the library and, in 1999, relocated to its final home in the former freight area (approximately five thousand square feet) within the historic Clarksdale Depot, built in 1918 for the Yazoo and Mississippi Valley Railroad. The museum's mission is to be a welcoming place celebrating blues history and heritage. It devotes itself to attaining and providing permanent and traveling exhibits related to groundbreaking blues artists hailing from the region. Among the highlights are life-size images of past blues musician icons. The Delta Blues Museum is a Mississippi Landmark property.

Delta Blues Museum. *Courtesy of Delta Blues Museum.*

Delta Blues Museum. *Courtesy of Amelia Delaney / Delta Blues Museum.*

Delta Blues Museum. *Courtesy of Ameliea Dulaney/Delta Blues Museum.*

Delta Children's Museum, Armitage Carousel. *Courtesy of the Delta Children's Museum.*

DELTA CHILDREN'S MUSEUM
E.E. BASS CENTER
323 SOUTH MAIN STREET
GREENVILLE, MS 38701

Although the Delta Children's Museum is not a structure, the organization provides educational programs, performances, exhibits and hands-on interactive learning to engage the children in arts activities and performances. It has been referred to as a "Museum without Walls." The museum outreaches to public schools to enhance the education of the underserved Delta student population and the region's highly regarded school system. The Delta Children's Museum also owns the Greenville Armitage Herschell Carousel (circa 1897–1901) in the E.E. Bass Cultural Arts Center, home to the Greenville Arts Council and other cultural organizations. The carousel arrived in Greenville in 1901 as "one of those steam-powered riding galleries they call carousels in Europe."

DESOTO COUNTY MUSEUM
111 EAST COMMERCE STREET
HERNANDO, MS 38632

The Historic DeSoto Foundation manages and operates the DeSoto County Museum, which opened in March 2003 to educate, preserve and interpret the county's history from 1541, during the time of Hernando de Soto's exploration, through the twentieth century using photos, documents and artifacts. The building looks more like a church in the rural South than a traditional cultural institution. Stepping inside, visitors see stuffed, life-sized animals native to the area and a mural reflecting DeSoto County's history. One section celebrates the Chickasaw and Choctaw Native American tribes that lived in and around Hernando. The importance of Jewish culture in DeSoto County is illustrated in another exhibit, *The Unknown Child*, which commemorates the 1.5 million children who died during the Holocaust. The museum hosts lectures and presentations.

EMMETT TILL HISTORIC INTREPID CENTER – E.T.H.I.C. MUSEUM
235 THOMAS STREET
GLENDORA, MS 38928

The Emmett Till Historic Intrepid Center is located approximately twenty miles from Money, Mississippi, where fourteen-year-old Emmett Till ventured into Bryant Grocery and Meat Market, which led to his brutal beating and death by Carolyn Bryant's husband, Roy, his half-brother J.W. Milam and a white mob after Carolyn claimed Till made advances at her. Till's lifeless body was tossed over the Black Bayou Bridge and found in the Tallahatchie River. The bridge once connected the town of Glendora to all the plantations north, south, east and west. The Intrepid Center is a small museum that highlights Emmett's life and death and the civil rights movement in Glendora, focusing on an unabashed accounting of the racism, terror and horror of bigotry. The E.T.H.I.C. museum opened in 2005 with the help and dedication of civil rights veteran Johnny B. Thomas, who continues to serve as mayor of Glendora after three decades of mayoral service. Thomas's father was one of five African American men listed as accomplices to the kidnapping and brutal murder of Emmett Till. To understand how Black people were forced to participate in perilous situations like this, one must understand how a voice, choice, opportunity and right to protest were nonexistent in the Jim Crow South. The museum educates visitors on other atrocities and situations that ushered in the civil rights era.

FIELDING L. WRIGHT ART CENTER / HOLCOMBE-NORWOOD HALL
DELTA STATE UNIVERSITY
1003 WEST SUNFLOWER ROAD
CLEVELAND, MS 38733

The Art Department in the Fielding L. Wright Art Center / Holcombe-Norwood Hall at Delta State University houses two art galleries and a permanent collection of impressive art by Salvador Dalí, Kathe Kollwitz, Leonard Baskin, Marie Hull, William Hollingsworth Jr., Walter Anderson and others. The building is named after Fielding Wright (1895–1956), who served as the forty-ninth and fiftieth governor of Mississippi and was the vice presidential nominee of the States' Rights Democratic Party alongside Strom Thurmond. A fervent supporter of Senator Theodore G. Bilbo, a member of the Ku Klux Klan, Wright fought to maintain racial segregation and circumvent civil rights legislation.

GATEWAY TO THE BLUES MUSEUM AND VISITORS CENTER
13625 HIGHWAY 61
TUNICA, MS 38664

This museum opened in February 2015 and presents over seven hundred items related to Mississippi's blues history. The 1895 train depot, donated by Mr. and Mrs. Edgar Hood, is a 3,500-square-foot exhibition space holding artifacts graciously loaned by Caesars Entertainment, which also donated the land. Along with artifacts initially housed at the Blues and Legends Hall of Fame Museum located at the Horseshoe Casino are interactive exhibits, artworks and a recording studio that teaches visitors about blues music and records blues songs. Five interactive galleries line the museum, each with a unique name: What Is Blues Music; Why Here, In the Mississippi Delta; Evolution of Style and Form; Evolution of the Guitar; and Blues Lyric Interactive. The museum "tells the story of the blues…in all its tormented and anguished glory," with curated exhibitions explaining the importance of the blues to the Delta and why it is America's "Gateway to the Blues." Displaying how African Americans toiled in the cotton fields and how their singing motivated their overworked, exhausted bodies and souls from generation to generation is part of the museum's mission.

GRAMMY MUSEUM MISSISSIPPI
800 SUNFLOWER ROAD
CLEVELAND, MS 38732

The Cleveland Music Foundation manages the GRAMMY Museum Mississippi, which opened in March 2016 and is affiliated with the GRAMMY Museum of Los Angeles, California. Mississippi is the first GRAMMY Museum location built outside of California. With its proximity along the Delta Blues Trail, its distance between Jackson and Memphis and its proximity to Delta State University—an essential resource and partner, especially to the DSU Music Institute and recording studio—the GRAMMY Museum Mississippi showcases "the Delta's rich musical heritage and the impact of that heritage across multiple musical genres" to "provide unique learning opportunities based on the enduring legacies of music in all forms." Many GRAMMY winners and lifetime achievement awardees are connected to Mississippi, which many say is the "Birthplace of America's Music." The GRAMMY Museum Mississippi exhibits that story by shedding light on the GRAMMY Awards and performance histories.

GREENVILLE AIR FORCE BASE MUSEUM
166 FIFTH AVENUE, SUITE 300
GREENVILLE MS 38701

Located inside the mezzanine level of the Mid-Delta Regional Airport, the Greenville Air Force Base Museum was initially the Greenville Army Airfield. This military base opened in August 1941 to train men and women and NATO (North Atlantic Treaty Organization) cadets as pilots, firefighters and emergency medical personnel. Military trainers hailed from as far away as Canada and Great Britain. The base permanently closed as a training facility in December 1960. But on January 31, 1966, seventy hungry, almost frozen African Americans protested at the facility for an agreeable economic pathway to employment, food and shelter, job training and land. From their meetings with the Student Nonviolent Coordinating Committee (SNCC), word was sent to President Lyndon B. Johnson to appeal to his efforts in the "War on Poverty" in their Jim Crow existence. Eventually, the African Americans were escorted off the base, but President Johnson released funds through the "Operation Help" program, and six months later, around five hundred thousand hungry people received food assistance. Still, state officials strongly opposed the enhanced preschool education and nutrition for African American children. The facility was then redeveloped as a regional airport. The Greenville community came together to preserve the Greenville Air Force Base story as a museum. They gathered artifacts, photos and other historical memorabilia of the men and women trainees at the airbase and designed the mezzanine level as a public museum. The museum pinpoints Greenville's aviation history and tells the incredible stories of those men and women trainees.

GREENVILLE HISTORY MUSEUM
409 WASHINGTON AVENUE
GREENVILLE, MS 38702

This venue is housed in the restored Miller Building, standing tightly between two other businesses. The outside sign reads "Greenville History Museum, Century in Review." Inside, visitors find a collection indicative of the area, like the photograph of Bonnie Parker and Clyde Barrow. The two once traveled through Greenville. Clyde wrote a letter to Henry Ford telling him how much he enjoyed driving the Ford V8. Among the exhibits are old jukeboxes, Victrolas and a Coke machine, pictures of local beauty queens, soldier uniforms, a potpourri of exciting history dating back at least one hundred years and a framed inspirational quote from Winston Churchill: "Success is not final, failure is not fatal. It is the courage to continue that counts." Curated to provide a unique glimpse into Greenville life from the late 1800s through the 1970s, the museum has a fascinating collection of memorabilia, artifacts, photographs and news clippings through each day of the historic Great Mississippi Flood of 1927 and other momentous events.

GREENWOOD BLUES HERITAGE MUSEUM AND GALLERY
222 HOWARD STREET
GREENWOOD, MS 38930

Visitors to Greenwood's Historic District may enjoy a guided tour of the district's points of interest, which includes sites related to the blues in the area, civil rights and the Civil War. The tour also includes cotton plantations, literary sites, Native American sites and the Greenwood Blues Heritage Museum and Gallery, which is located on the second floor of the Three Deuces Building (erected in 1900), just above the Blue Parrot Restaurant and Veronica's Custom Bakery. The facility was the former home of WGRM gospel radio station, where Riley "B.B." King sang and played on air with the Famous St. John's Gospel Singers. (See *The Life and Legacy of B.B. King: A Mississippi Blues Icon* by Diane Williams.) Established and incorporated in 2000, the museum celebrates Robert Johnson with a mission to increase awareness and emphasize the importance of blues history in America. Steve Levere, a fan of Johnson, owns the museum's artifacts and memorabilia celebrating regional blues musicians, WGRM and local history.

HIGHWAY 61 BLUES MUSEUM
307 NORTH BROAD STREET
LELAND, MS 38756

Located in the old Montgomery Hotel Building is the Highway 61 Blues Museum, which honors musicians from the Mississippi Delta. On each side of the gated entry are colorful murals, one of blues musicians and the other of the Delta and its people. Visitors in May can join the crowd attending the Leland Crawfish Festival. In September, the Frog Festival is held. But at any

Highway 61 Blues Museum. *Courtesy of Diane Williams.*

time visitors might meet Raymond "Pat" Thomas, the son of the legendary James "Son" Thomas. Pat may render a tune and offer a collectible domino die on which he draws his signature art designs.

JAKETOWN MUSEUM
116 WEST JACKSON STREET
BELZONI, MS 39038

The Jaketown Museum provides visitors with education on prehistoric civilization and culture and paints a picture of the earliest inhabitants of North America. It also preserves the history and artifacts of the mounds created by the early Native Americans before the Choctaw and Chickasaw Nations. Artifacts include arrowheads, red jasper beads and hematite plummets acquired via trade. The museum displays some of the earliest Native American earthworks. The mounds are located four miles north of Belzoni on Highway 7 in Humphreys County. Built during the late Archaic Poverty Point Period (1700–800 BCE) by various tribes, these sacred man-made landforms served multiple purposes, some representing burial grounds with traditional rituals and rites of passage. Others represented temple gathering sites. Only three of the original eighteen mounds are visible today due to human manipulation, such as farming. The mound site is listed as a National Historic Landmark.

JIM HENSON DELTA BOYHOOD MUSEUM
  (THE BIRTHPLACE OF KERMIT THE FROG)
415 SOUTH DEER CREEK DRIVE EAST
LELAND, MS 39649

Leland is the "Birthplace of the Frog" and the childhood home of Jim Henson. The museum is located in the former chamber of commerce building along the Deer Creek. Behind the building is a bridge called the Rainbow Connection. The Jim Henson Delta Boyhood Museum has one and a half gallery space rooms and a gift shop that carries T-shirts and Muppet-related items. Exhibits include sketches, concept art, finished pieces, Muppet characters from years of television production, photographs of Jim Henson and his family and Henson's work. The bridge derives its name from "The Rainbow Connection," a song written by Paul Williams and Kenny Ascher for Kermit the Frog's first Muppet movie. Visiting the museum during the Frog Festival in September is a way to be immersed in a community that enjoys everything about "the frog."

Jim Henson Delta Boyhood Museum. *Courtesy of Mary Beth Magee.*

KATE FREEMAN CLARK ART GALLERY
300 EAST COLLEGE AVENUE
HOLLY SPRINGS, MS 38635

The Kate Freeman Clark Art Gallery, a "fine and social arts museum," opened in 1963. The gallery storage room contains the remainder of Clark's 1,200 paintings, drawings and watercolors. Three rooms in the Kate Freeman Clark Art Gallery have her paintings and a few by her beloved instructor, William Merritt Chase. Originally from Holly Springs, Mississippi, Kate Freeman Clark (1875–1957) was widely known for her plein air paintings, which she signed "Freeman Clark" or "K. Freeman Clark" so her gender was not easily identified. Women were not highly regarded as artists at the turn of the twentieth century. Clark left Mississippi early on to hone her craft, and it was not until her death that her 1,200 paintings received deserved recognition. A well-trained visual artist, Kate had a career that spanned twenty years, which she gave up when her grandmother passed away and Kate returned to Holly Springs.

She bequeathed hundreds of her paintings and provided the funding to build a museum to house and curate her work, encompassing landscapes, portraits and still life, with some images six feet in height. The Marshall County Historical Museum stores the artist's papers, jewelry, dresses, photographs and other artifacts.

MARSHALL COUNTY HISTORICAL MUSEUM
220 EAST COLLEGE AVENUE
HOLLY SPRINGS, MS 38635

In 1970, the Marshall County Historical Society led the charge to create the Marshall County Historical Museum, now fifty years old. The Museum resides in the 1903 building formerly known as Mississippi Synodical College, which operated until 1939 and is listed in the National Register of Historic Places. Three floors of exhibit space display items relating to Marshall County, including a collection of military uniforms, 1920s flapper-girl clothing and a taxidermy of native regional animals.

The Marshall County Historical Society displays its collection of Native American artifacts, quilts, old advertisements, antique books, old bottles, dollhouses and dollhouse villages, sports memorabilia, promotional materials from past presidential campaigns, flags, weapons, paintings, an antique

Victrola and a Victorian children's book collection. The museum earned the nickname "Grandmother's Attic" due to the many treasures donated by Marshall County residents. Items that belonged to Kate Freeman Clark are also at the museum. (See also the Kate Freeman Clark Art Gallery).

MARTIN AND SUE KING RAILROAD HERITAGE MUSEUM
115 SOUTH BAYOU AVENUE
CLEVELAND, MS 38732

The City of Cleveland owns the Martin and Sue King Railroad Heritage Museum, which preserves and promotes the history and culture of the railroad and the impact it has made on the Mississippi Delta. Built in 1884, the rail tracks no longer line the streets. The last train whistled through in 1995. Cleveland mayor Martin T. King desired to preserve the heritage and importance of rail transport and opened the Martin and Sue King Railroad Heritage Museum in 2009 in downtown Cleveland. The facility houses one of the most extensive three-rail O-gauge model train layouts in the Southeast, measuring seventy-one by seventeen feet. It is home to artifacts capturing the history of the railroad industry. The 1941 Illinois Central caboose displays memorabilia, photos, documents and tools used by rail crews known as "Gandy Dancers," a nickname for men working in synchronized, unified rhythm and movement patterns that encouraged more energy to do the job. Periodically, museum exhibitions change and range from early rail and timber to the blues music created around life, living and traveling the rails.

MERRILL MUSEUM
601 EAST JACKSON STREET
CARROLLTON, MS 38917

Captain Charles Connell built the two-story Merrill's General Store in 1834, the year Carrollton became a town. Initially, it was a mercantile store, but the painted sign on the side of the building reveals it evolved into the Carrollton Coffin & Furniture Co., Springs, Mattresses, where customers have "All Calls Promptly Answered, Day or Night." The building, now owned by the Carroll County Society for the Preservation of Antiquities, was renovated in 2009 as a museum. Displays honor the family of Arizona senator John Sidney McCain III, who were early settlers. The senator's great-grandfather

Merrill Museum. *Courtesy of Richelle Putnam.*

once served as sheriff and supervisor. The McCain family donated treasured memorabilia, including a picture of John McCain as a child sitting on his grandfather's knee. Exhibits incorporate collections of arrowheads, antique bottles, toys, old military uniforms, awards, plaques, military personnel pictures, portraits, notes, copies of speeches and information on Carrollton native and writer Elizabeth Spencer (1921–2019). On the building lot are two historical markers: a Mississippi Literary Trail marker celebrating Spencer and a Mississippi Country Music Trail marker commemorating Narmour and Smith, a popular old-time string band in the 1920s and 1930s. The museum opens during the Carrollton Pilgrimage and Pioneer Day Festival in October. Otherwise, it is open by appointment only.

MISSISSIPPI WILDLIFE HERITAGE MUSEUM
302 NORTH BROAD STREET
LELAND, MS 38756

The Mississippi Wildlife Foundation opened the Mississippi Wildlife Heritage Museum, a fifteen-thousand-square-foot facility, in June 2017. Its mission is to preserve the history, heritage and traditions of hunting, fishing and the great outdoors and to honor its participants and educate the public on Mississippi's vast natural resources. Exhibits consist of three thousand vintage photos, hunting gear, firearms, saddles, deer heads, game animals, local duck and turkey calls, boats, outboards, fishing rods and hunting clothing. Within the Mississippi Outdoor Hall of Fame is the name Holt Collier, the hunting guide and former enslaved African American who guided Theodore Roosevelt on his Mississippi Delta hunt. There is also a gift shop.

MOUND BAYOU MUSEUM OF AFRICAN AMERICAN CULTURE AND HISTORY
200 ROOSEVELT STREET
MOUND BAYOU, MS 38762

The Mound Bayou Museum opened in 2021, during the height of the world's coronavirus pandemic, and was the idea of Harmon Johnson Jr., a Jackson State University graduate and history major. The museum displays how the town of Mound Bayou, founded in 1887 and incorporated in 1898, was settled by former enslaved African Americans in Bolivar County. Early 1800 Mound Bayou landowner Joseph E. Davis, brother of President Jefferson Davis, encouraged the enslaved people on his plantation to thrive by teaching them basic skills. Today, the town consists of 561 acres of land and maintains its remarkable history of pride through the work of this museum. The plethora of photos and artifacts tells stories of the valiant men and women of the civil rights movement and reflects on the blues and blues musicians. The website showcases multiple videos that bring Mound Bayou, its people and their culture to life.

MUSEUM OF THE MISSISSIPPI DELTA
1608 US HIGHWAY 82
GREENWOOD, MS 38930

Formerly known as Cottonlandia, the Museum of the Mississippi Delta was founded in 1969 and tells the story of the Delta. Plows, fertilizer spreaders, mule hams, blacksmith items and even century-old rudimentary tools used for pulling teeth fill one expansive room. In other rooms, visitors discover another portion of Leflore County's past through artifacts and furniture from Malmaison, the home of Greenwood LeFlore and the community's military history through a collection of uniforms, veteran's lists, posters, Civil War canon and a model of the battle of nearby Fort Pemberton. The museum houses an ample collection of Native American trade beads, arrowheads and other materials of Mississippi Delta history dating back to CE 1400–1600. Within this museum, visitors find a sense of the Mississippi Delta community and region.

1927 FLOOD MUSEUM
118 SOUTH HINDS STREET
GREENVILLE, MS 38701

The 1927 Flood Museum is housed in the oldest structure in downtown Greenville, a red-brick building on South Hinds between Main Street and Washington Avenue. Its mission is to share the storied history of the Great Mississippi Flood of 1927 that affected twenty-seven thousand square miles. After hefty rainfall during the summer of 1926, the Mississippi River's floodwaters rose to thirty feet, swelling its tributaries into surrounding states and making Mississippi one of the most devastated places along the Mississippi River. In all, 640,000 people were affected. The water converged over Greenville, causing the loss of agriculture, livestock, homes and human lives. The incident kept African American laborers from leaving the state, encouraging the Great Migration. The museum also reveals what happened to the levee at Stops Landing, eight miles north of Greenville. Exhibits of artifacts and photographs show the flood-ravaged area, and the museum's short documentary brings to life the flood that impacted Arkansas, Louisiana, Missouri, Illinois, Kansas, Tennessee, Kentucky, Oklahoma and Texas and was one of America's most horrendous natural disasters.

her quote, "I'm sick and tired of being sick and tired." Pictorial exhibits at the museum reference the life work and efforts in the cause of humanity of these two important people.

## RIVER ROAD QUEEN WELCOME CENTER AND MUSEUM OF THE DELTA
## 1572 US 278 (1512 HIGHWAY 82 AT WEST REED ROAD)
## GREENVILLE, MS 38704

Travelers find the River Road Queen Welcome Center and Museum of the Delta in an 1800s replica riverboat shaped like a paddle steamer on the Great River Road along the Mississippi River just south of downtown Greenville. The Welcome Center provides the history of the Delta region and Washington County community. The second-floor museum contains exhibits including river artifacts and items related to the Delta region, such as cotton, blues musicians, writers, the great river flood, Kermit the Frog (the product of Jim Henson of Leland, Mississippi), the Great River Road and cemeteries. The River Road Queen Welcome Center hosts presentations and events all year, and the building is a must-see attraction, as the boat was part of the State of Mississippi Pavilion exhibition during the 1984 New Orleans World's Fair.

## RUST COLLEGE, ROY WILKINS COLLECTION AT THE LEONTYNE PRICE LIBRARY
## 150 RUST AVENUE
## HOLLY SPRINGS, MS 38635

The Methodist Episcopal Church missionaries established Rust College in 1866. Constructed in 1970, the Leontyne Price Library, named after Mississippi's own Mary Violet Leontyne Price, a world-famous African American opera singer, is in the center of the campus. The third floor is home to significant collections of art and archives, as well as books, microfilms, records, tapes, CDs, DVDs, periodicals, news articles, the history of the United Methodist and the Roy Ottoway Wilkins collection from the former executive secretary of the National Association for the Advancement of Colored People (NAACP). The International Culture Room contains a collection of artifacts and printed materials representing faculty and staff travels to West Africa, Denmark, Norway, Pakistan, India, China, Mexico, Egypt, Israel, Tibet and the United States. Also showcased are handmade dolls, clothing, jewelry, instruments, sculptures and other items from West Africa and an Inuit Pre-Columbian art collection.

Tate County Heritage Museum
201 South Ward Street
Senatobia, MS 38668

The Tate County Heritage Museum inhabits the historic Tate County Courthouse, built around 1875, with additions and remodeling in 1904, 1975 and 1999. Under the front sidewalk is a time capsule. Its identifying marker reads, "Time Capsule, Tate County, 1873–1998, Open 2098." When the capsule is finally opened, inside will be found a copy of a special edition of the *Democrat* newspaper, a Bible, a phone book, a one-dollar bill and a book about the county. The courthouse, listed as a Mississippi Historic Landmark in the National Register of Historic Places, has been honored with a marker because of its preservation efforts regarding the life of early settlers, their community and their military service. Along the courthouse corridors, visitors enjoy pictures and memorabilia related to Tate County, which includes Senatobia, Arkabutla, Independence and Coldwater. The Heritage Museum Foundation of Tate County office manages the museum.

Tunica Museum
1 Museum Boulevard
Tunica, MS 38676

The Tunica Museum in downtown Tunica serves as caretaker to the Tate Log House, an 1840s dogtrot-style log cabin, the oldest known edifice in the county. In 1997, five individuals determined that Tunica County's history should be preserved and displayed. The downtown museum boasts 6,500 square feet of permanent exhibit space highlighting wildlife that inhabits the area, Indian mounds, folk life, social activities, archaeology and 1,600 square feet of space for temporary exhibits. The Tunica Indians once thrived in the area, and visitors learn about the Native Americans, particularly the Chickasaw, who preceded the colonial era in America. The museum also illustrates what life was like for African Americans enslaved on plantations before and after the Civil War. The museum reflects on the early Spanish exploration of Hernando de Soto and how the gaming industry changed the landscape and brought jobs and entertainment to Tunica. It also tells Mississippi's segregation story, the fight against the boll weevil, the Great Mississippi Flood of 1927 and the loss of field workers during the Great Migration. An encompassing nature trail celebrates the landscape's positive aspects.

TUNICA RIVERPARK MUSEUM
1 RIVER PARK DRIVE
ROBINSONVILLE, MS 38864

Not too far from the casinos, overlooking the Mississippi River, the Tunica RiverPark Museum explores the Delta's rich history and the Mississippi River, housing artifacts and curated history of nature, wildlife and flora inside and outside, as well as four aquariums with all types of fish, turtles and more. The museum includes interactive permanent and temporary exhibits reflecting the community's long history of Spanish explorers, the Great Mississippi Flood of 1927 and the Natives who first inhabited and cared for the land.

WINTERVILLE MOUNDS AND MUSEUM
415 HIGHWAY 1 NORTH
GREENVILLE, MS 38703

Named for the nearby town of Winterville, the mounds and museum on Mississippi Highway 1, six miles north of Highway 82 and Highway 1 in Greenville, were designated a National Historic Landmark in 1993. The museum resembles an Indian mound on the outside. Since CE 1200–1250, the twelve Indian mounds, with the largest being a fifty-five-foot-tall temple mound, elevated parts of the flat Delta landscape. The site was dedicated as a Mississippi State Park and is maintained by the Mississippi Department of Archives and History. The Winterville Mounds, originally twenty-three mounds, served to celebrate cultural traditions and sacred activities for the Chickasaw and Choctaw Native Americans. (For more information on Indian mounds, refer to the entry on the Jaketown Museum.) Exhibits tell the story of the continent's earliest civilization—who, what, where, when and how—and there is a diverse collection of archaeological artifacts, pottery vessels, earthworks, stone tools and ornaments. The museum also exhibits the history of the area.

WROX Museum
257 Delta Avenue
Clarksdale MS 38614

WROX bears the mark of time and history. The station is legendary for having had the foresight to engage world-famous artists, and its 257 Delta Avenue location is in the National Register of Historic Places and boasts a Mississippi Blues Trail marker. The station hosted many well-known artists such as Sonny Boy Williamson II, Sam Cook, B.B. King, Little Milton, Pinetop Perkins, Elvis Presley, Charley Pride, Bobby Rush, Rufus Thomas and Muddy Waters. Ike Turner became a station disc jockey and hosted his show, *Jive Till Five*, transmitted on WROX AM. In 2004, WROX opened as a museum exhibiting testaments to what the station has achieved and displays records, record players, radios, pictures, handwritten notes, newspaper articles, a jukebox, 45s (records), microphones, posters and station schedules. Today's WROX format is oldies on 105.7 FM.

Yellow Fever Martyrs Church & Museum
305 East College Avenue
Holly Springs, MS 38635

The Yellow Fever Martyrs Church & Museum was constructed in 1842 as the Christ Episcopal Church and later served as St. Joseph Catholic Church. In 2000, the Historic Heritage Preservation Corporation established the Yellow Fever Martyrs Church & Museum to explore and preserve the history of the yellow fever epidemic. At this writing, it is the only museum dedicated to how yellow fever impacted regions of the United States. Holly Springs survived the Civil War, but the epidemic killed three hundred residents and almost destroyed the town. The museum focuses on the valiant efforts of the church to care for Holly Springs residents. Exhibits include pictures of the original building design and memorials of the epidemic's martyrs. Other artifacts protected in glass display cases are documents referencing the epidemic. One room is set up as a field hospital. A delightful highlight is the Michelly Painting, a portrait of Christ at the Crucifixion made around 1858. The museum hosts lectures and films, and the structure is a historic landmark.

Part II

# NORTHEAST MISSISSIPPI

American Indian Artifacts Museum
179 State Line Road
Columbus, MS 39702

The American Indian Artifacts Museum exhibits items from hundreds and thousands of years ago. Local Native Americans have also donated to the museum.

Apron Museum
110 West Eastport Street
Iuka, MS 38852

Established in 2006, the Apron Museum exhibits and sells aprons, tablecloths, vintage linen, cotton, gingham, quilts and flour sacks. Clothespins clip a multitude of colorful aprons in various styles on clotheslines, some appliqued, some embroidered and adorned with bows, ruffles and pockets, most in cotton or linen. Each represents a time in history and the person who wore it—a nurse during the American Civil War, blacksmith, cook, chef, butcher, carpenter, painter, printer, shopkeeper or homemaker. All wore aprons, whether to protect clothing or dress it up. The museum has upward of four thousand aprons and is a one-room showcase with aprons dating back to the Civil War and from as far away as Australia. This museum, which may very well be the only apron museum in the United States, has been featured in *Ripley's Believe It or Not!*

## Black History Museum of Corinth
### 1109 Meigg Street
### Corinth, MS 38834

Located in a house once owned by William Dakota Webb (1893–1975) and Adrienne Combs Webb (1896–1987), the Black History Museum of Corinth dedicates itself to identifying, preserving, curating and promoting the heritage and lives of the area's African Americans. Civil rights memorabilia, religious and educational items and donations from Corinth residents are incorporated into the displays. One section celebrates Roy Allen "Bo Peep" Robinson and his days with the Tuskegee Airmen as an aerial photographer flying reconnaissance missions over North Africa and Europe in planes piloted by the famous airmen. Antiquated straw fans, folk art, an African facemask, pictures and newspaper articles are displayed. Various rooms include school artifacts, memorabilia, information on community churches and military service members. The famous Ruby Elzy, a soprano singer and native of Pontotoc, is highlighted. There is also an exhibition depicting Rosa Parks's life.

## Borroum's Drug Store and Soda Fountain
### 604 East Waldron Street
### Corinth, MS 38834

In Corinth, Mississippi, Borroum's Drug Store and Soda Fountain is a popular tourist attraction. It is the oldest drugstore in the state and the oldest family-owned drugstore in the country, established in 1865 by Andrew Jackson "Jack" Borroum. Museum exhibits inside the drugstore include original cobalt-blue dispensing bottles with gold-leaf medicinal labels written in Latin, pharmaceutical scales with amethyst balances, medicines, antique paraphernalia including a tiny midwife spoon for measuring, fixtures, photographs from early Corinth, memorabilia, Civil War relics, Native American arrowheads and a 1926 cash register. The fully functioning soda fountain serves Corinth's famous delicacy, the slug burger, as well as other menu items at its Art Deco bar. The burger's name evolved from the Great Depression, because the burger, made of beef, filler, pickles, onions and mustard, cost a "slug," which was a nickel.

BRICE'S CROSS ROADS NATIONAL BATTLEFIELD
CROSSROADS VISITORS AND MISSISSIPPI FINAL STANDS INTERPRETIVE CENTER
607 GRISHAM STREET
BALDWYN, MS 38824

The Civil War Board operates Brice's Cross Roads National Battlefield. The museum inside the Visitors and Mississippi Final Stands Interpretive Center expounds on the history of the Civil War, specifically when Nathan Bedford Forrest and others directed a campaign at Brice's Cross Roads. A thirty-minute video explains the battle near Tupelo, Mississippi, and the exhibits, clearly displayed with dioramas and period artifacts, reflect the battle's history. Exhibitions include the war's pertinent timeline, books and various flags. Artifacts include rifles, barrels, stirrups, mule shoes, a soldier's pocket watch, a canister shot, supplies for William Tecumseh Sherman's soldiers and a campaign timeline of Confederate and Union forces. The Battle of Brice's Crossroads, fought July 13–15, 1864, was one of Major General Forrest's great Civil War victories. Also fought on those dates was the Battle of Harrisburg / Old Town Creek, whose history is also recorded on-site. Almost one hundred soldiers are laid to rest in the battlefield cemetery.

BRUCE FORESTRY MUSEUM
109 PUBLIC SQUARE
BRUCE, MS 38915

The Bruce Chamber of Commerce created the Bruce Forestry Museum in the E.L. Bruce Company General Store building to highlight the history of logging and the town of Bruce, situated along the Skuna River in Calhoun County. Exhibits include a rope-driven steam engine, a restored log wagon, tools, equipment, works by local artists and early photographs of Bruce. The restored Bruce building earned Mississippi Main Street's "Best Façade Renovation" award.

## Burns-Belfry Museum & Multicultural Center
## 710 East Jackson Avenue
## Oxford, MS 38655

A National Trust for Historic Preservation site, the Burns-Belfry Museum is in the former Burns Methodist Episcopal Church building, erected in 1910, across the street from the Lafayette County Jail and not too far from Oxford Square. The original wooden house of worship was built around 1867 by freed African Americans in Oxford in an area once known as Freedmen Town. The Oxford–Lafayette County Heritage Foundation (OLCHF) and Oxford Development Association work to facilitate the museum's activities. The OLCHF strives to save buildings destined for abolishment and is dedicated to the community's African American history. Museum exhibits provide a visual experience depicting the African American story from enslavement through the civil rights era. An interpretive exhibit is a humanities reflection on life and community.

## Casey Jones Railroad Museum
## 105 Railroad Avenue
## Water Valley, MS 38965

The Casey Jones Railroad Museum lives in a reconstructed railroad building in downtown Water Valley. The two-room museum tells the story of heroic railroad engineer Casey Jones. A mannequin dressed as a railroad employee in the center of the room likely represents Jones. Displays include a three-cent postage stamp created in his honor and the cracked and battered bell from Jones's doomed train ride. Other items include the Bruce Garner Collection of Memorabilia, donated items from former employees of the Illinois Central Railroad, photographs and documents.

Casey Jones Railroad Museum. *Courtesy of Diane Williams.*

## Charles H. Templeton, Sr. Music Museum
Mitchell Memorial Library, fourth floor
Mississippi State University (MSU)
395 Hardy Road
Mississippi State (Starkville), MS 39762

The mission of the Charles H. Templeton, Sr. Music Museum is to tell the story of the "business of music," the moods music generates and the influence on today's music. Starkville businessman Charles H. Templeton was a 1949 graduate of Mississippi State University who collected gramophones, player pianos, music boxes, a harp, sheet music representing various music eras, a Regina Hexaphone and other musical instruments and recordings. The collection explores the music industry's progression in the 1800s and 1900s and includes one of the most complete collections of Victor Talking Machines (1897–1930). The Mississippi State University library location produces, preserves and provides access to digital collections that support teaching and research through sheet music, diaries, correspondence, ledgers, photographs, transcripts, publications and other materials through its digital collections. The library also hosts the annual Charles Templeton Ragtime Jazz Festival, which includes concerts, seminars and tours of the museum.

## Chickasaw County Heritage Museum
304 East Woodland Circle
Houston, MS 38851

In Joe Brigance Memorial Park in Houston, Mississippi, visitors find the Chickasaw County Heritage Museum, managed by the Chickasaw County Heritage and Genealogical Society. The museum preserves the history of the city, county and the South with artifacts and memorabilia highlighting everything from war heroes to culture. An agricultural exhibit building with farm implements and equipment dates to a time before technology made things easier. There is a genealogy center and research library for the study of folklife relating to the contributions of citizens, both past and present, where visitors can uncover family history through documents, records and photographs. A historic blues marker in front highlights the life and work of guitarist Booker "Bukka" T. Washington White, who was born in Houston.

## THE CITY OF AMORY REGIONAL MUSEUM
## 801 SOUTH THIRD STREET
## AMORY, MS 38821

The City of Amory Regional Museum reflects regional history and is housed in the century-old Gilmore Sanitarium, listed as a Mississippi Historic Landmark. Philanthropist E.G. Gilmore gifted the building to the city, and it served as a convalescent nursing home for four years in the early 1960s before becoming the Amory Regional Museum in 1976. The Friends of the Amory Regional Museum facilitate the museum's activities, like quilt exhibitions. Museum collections include equipment used by the early sanitarium and a debutant dress, reflecting the vibrancy of Amory's citizens. The museum celebrates local, regional and national artists and has a quaint gift shop. The building is said to be haunted by the former sanitarium doctor, Dr. M.Q. Ewing, hospital chief of staff.

## COBB ARCHAEOLOGY MUSEUM / COBB INSTITUTE OF ARCHAEOLOGY
## MISSISSIPPI STATE UNIVERSITY
## 206 COBB BUILDING
## 340 LEE BOULEVARD
## MISSISSIPPI STATE (STARKVILLE), MS 39762

The Cobb Archaeology Museum in the basement of the Cobb Institute of Archaeology on the campus of Mississippi State University dedicates itself "to provide sponsorship and support for research, outreach and instructional programs related to the Middle Eastern origins of Western Civilization and to the Indians of the South, particularly in Mississippi." Cully Alton Cobb (1884–1975) and Lois Dowdle Cobb (1889–1987) founded the institute in 1971 to be the research and service unit of the College of Arts & Sciences with efforts directed to "the specific purposes of archaeological research, study, travel, excavations and explorations, publications and reports, and other similar uses or purposes." The collection of over five thousand objects from around the world is contained in the Lois Dowdle Cobb Museum, with an artifact collection, multiple laboratories, classrooms, office spaces and a library.

Columbus War Museum
1501 Main Street
Columbus, MS 39701

The Columbus War Museum celebrates veterans and those who died fighting in various military battles. The museum exhibits pictures and memorabilia representing the courage and sacrifice of service members from various branches of the United States military. The museum is also a gathering place for veterans.

Corinth Civil War Interpretive Center
501 West Linden Street
Corinth, MS 38834

In 2004, the National Park Service established a state-of-the-art, fifteen-thousand-square-foot Corinth Civil War Interpretive Center to focus on the war in Northeast Mississippi and to provide a comprehensive accounting of the Battle of Shiloh and the siege, occupation and Battle of Corinth. The museum thoughtfully presents the African American experience during the war and contains information on the Corinth Contraband Camp (see entry of the same name). Displays and exhibits provide the causes of the war to enhance a deeper understanding. Throughout the facility, video rooms and audio phones provide additional information on the Confederate retreat to Corinth, the Union siege of the city and the Battle, which was an attempt to retake the city. The museum also includes a recounting of what it was like in the contraband camp, which grew to the size of a small city. The indoor information panels, dioramas and artifacts complement the powerful outdoor exhibits, which includes a water memorial, the Stream of American History, symbolizing various Civil War battles and the thirteen colonies. There is also a garden with a reflecting pond.

Corinth Coca-Cola Museum
305 Waldron Street
Corinth, MS 38834

The Coca-Cola Museum, in an old wooden building in downtown Corinth, is a four-generation, family-owned franchise that opened in 1906. It was originally named Coca-Cola Bottling Works, and franchises grew from six service facilities to franchises throughout Mississippi, Tennessee, Arkansas and Missouri. The museum's motto is "faith, vision, investment, and hard work," and it refers to the drink as "Happiness in a Bottle." The common belief is that the term *pop* originated in Mississippi. Inside the museum, visitors find Coca-Cola memorabilia and collectibles, drink and vending machines, signage, toy delivery vans and toy eight-wheelers, a cooler, a radio and anniversary (1907–82) and centennial (2007) bottles. Also included are Hutchinson bottles (1894–1903), a logo clock and thermometer, the Vienna Art Plate (circa 1908–12) and a unique metal sign of a woman in a bathtub that reads, "Appearances are sometimes deceiving, but Coca-Cola can always be relied on as naturally refreshing and exhilarating."

CORINTH CONTRABAND CAMP
902 NORTH PARKWAY STREET
CORINTH, MS 38834

The Corinth Contraband Camp is one of 562 camps where African American enslaved people sought freedom and protection after the Civil War and learned cooperative farming, reading and essential independence. With the passing of the Emancipation Proclamation in January 1863, a contraband camp was established in Union-occupied Corinth, Mississippi, which grew to around six thousand people, comparable to a city. This outdoor museum exhibits slave monuments, including the bronze statue *Woman and Child Reading* and six life-size bronze sculptures depicting a laundress, a (white) chaplain and a (Black) boy, a farmer and a "Leaning Woman" standing with hands on hips leaning with back against a structure. Plaques are strategically placed to commemorate the significance of the camp.

(CRAIG AND ELAINE VECHNORIK'S) BENCH MARK WORKS LLC
    MOTORCYCLE MUSEUM
3400 EARLE FORKS ROAD
STURGIS, MS 39769

The mission of Bench Mark Works is to restore vintage BMW motorcycles. The Bench Mark Works LLC Motorcycle Museum contains Craig

Vechnorik's collection and is a great place to buy hard-to-find motorcycle parts. Craig Vechnorik offers valuable technical advice on parts and motorcycle repair. Bench Mark is also a Streib and Ural sidecar dealer.

CROSSROADS MUSEUM AND THE HISTORIC CORINTH DEPOT
221 NORTH FILLMORE STREET
CORINTH, MS 38834

This museum celebrates Corinth, Mississippi, also known as the Crossroads of the South, founded by Houston Mitchell and Hamilton Mask in 1854. More than a dozen exhibits cover famous local people, local delicacies and how the railroads once operated as the primary transportation in America. Other exhibits display Corinth's prehistory and geology, how natural landmarks shaped the city and artifacts from the Chickasaw Tribe, some of the first people to settle the area. Among those highlighted are aviation pioneer Roscoe Turner; Major League Baseball star Don Blasingame, who was born and raised in Corinth; and National Football League great Jackie Simpson. There is also a gift shop and a research library, and outside is a vintage train caboose and Civil War cannon used during the Battle of Shiloh.

CULLIS & GLADYS WADE CLOCK MUSEUM
MISSISSIPPI STATE UNIVERSITY
75 B.S. HOOD DRIVE
MISSISSIPPI STATE (STARKVILLE), MS 39759

On the Mississippi State University campus inside of the Cullis Wade Depot, the Cullis & Gladys Wade Clock Museum showcases over four hundred clocks representing extraordinary artisan craftsmanship, fine motor coordination and high-quality woodworking. Cullis Wade and Gladys Valentine Wade found a common interest in collecting clocks, and their collection represents many recognized names in clockmaking and manufacturing. Each clock is curated with a small plaque that lists the type, vintage, manufacturer and description.

DREAM RIDERZ CLASSIC CARS & COLLECTIBLES
913 US 45 NORTH
CORINTH, MS 38834

Located outside of Corinth, a few miles south of where US45 and US72 meet, Ethan Rider planned the opening of a museum complete with classic cars, motorcycles, tanks, a historic fire truck, muscle cars and an antique Ford Model A. The collection represents vehicles from the 1920s to the present. Inside of the twenty-thousand-square-foot facility, visitors will find upward of eighty vehicles, but there are over two hundred in the collection, with five vehicles rotating from storage into the showroom every month. The cars are handsomely displayed with identifying placards. The museum opened in 2019 and is privately owned. This classic car museum came on the scene a few short months after the Tupelo Automobile Museum closed. In fact, Dream Riderz was able to obtain eight vehicles from the Tupelo collection.

DUNN-SEILER GEOLOGY MUSEUM
108 HILBUN HALL
MISSISSIPPI STATE (STARKVILLE), MS 39762

The Dunn-Seiler Geology Museum in the Department of Geosciences at Mississippi State University is named after Dr. Paul Heaney Dunn and Mr. Franklin Carl Seiler. Founded in 1946, the museum preserves specimens collected from students, faculty and donors and aims to educate, inform, display and encourage best practices, promoting public literacy about geology and earth science. The facility has an extensive collection of minerals and specimens, including a triceratops skull cast, a Cretaceous crocodile skull, displays of mass extinctions, asteroid specimens and many other geological finds. Some of the items in the collection date back to the late 1800s. There is also an overview of the geologic history of Mississippi. Each year, the museum celebrates National Fossil Day, Earth Day and Darwin Day and hosts recycling competitions.

(ELVIS) PRESLEY HEIGHTS MUSEUM
100 BRIAR RIDGE ROAD
TUPELO, MS 38802

An area of the Presley Heights Museum focuses on Elvis Presley, with memorabilia and other items, but the museum primarily presents the history of Tupelo, Mississippi, and the world.

EUGENIA SUMMERS GALLERY AND MUW FINE ART GALLERY
1100 COLLEGE STREET MUW-70
COLUMBUS, MS 39701

The Eugenia Summers Gallery is on the Mississippi University for Women (the W) campus in Columbus, Mississippi, at Summer Hall, home to the Department of Art and Design. Three galleries are the Ralph Hudson Art Gallery, the Eugenia Summers Gallery and the permanent art collection. Art also hangs along the corridor walls. The permanent collection includes prints, African masks, southern art, Mississippi art and faculty artworks from the twentieth and twenty-first centuries in an exhibit titled *Looking Back*. The galleries host evolving contemporary exhibitions throughout the year.

FRANK AND VIRGINIA WILLIAMS COLLECTION OF LINCOLNIANA GALLERY
MITCHELL MEMORIAL LIBRARY, FOURTH AND FIFTH FLOORS
MISSISSIPPI STATE UNIVERSITY
395 HARDY ROAD
MISSISSIPPI STATE (STARKVILLE), MS 39762

The Mitchell Memorial Library is home to the largest repository of privately held materials related to Abraham Lincoln, the sixteenth president of the United States. Frank J. Williams began his collection as a child. In 2017, he donated his collection, which included documents, books, artifacts, paintings and more, known as the Lincolniana Collection. Frank J. Williams was a chief justice in Rhode Island who authored several books related to Abraham Lincoln and Ulysses S. Grant and was the recipient of the prestigious Jurist of the Year Award. Virginia Williams was a schoolteacher who taught overseas for the U.S. Department of Defense. Newspaper articles, magazines, journals, original letters and legal documents that reference Abraham Lincoln have been cataloged and are available for research.

FRENCH CAMP HISTORIC AREA
234 LEFLEUR CIRCLE
FRENCH CAMP, MS 39745

On the 440-mile Natchez Trace, the pioneer trail connecting people between Natchez, Mississippi, and Nashville, Tennessee, the French Camp Academy, established in 1812, is a quaint village offering a visitor's center, a museum, a gift shop, Children of God Pottery Studio (with a resident potter on-site), a restaurant, a thrift shop and a boardwalk winding through the camp. The bed-and-breakfast community contains three cabins: the main B&B, the B&B Jr. and the Burford Cabin. Other historic buildings include the Colonel James Drane House (circa 1846), listed in the National Register of Historic Places; the LeFlore Carriage House; a blacksmith Shop; a sorghum mill; the French Camp Log Cabin Museum; and the Bread Bakery. The Huffman Log Cabin Gift Shop sells locally made products like molasses, sweet onion pecan dressing and freshly baked bread. Hand-crafted merchandise includes beautiful Amish-made rocking chairs, items made by craftsmen and students, quilts and other unique items. Council House Cafe connects to the gift shop, and both support school programs and ministries. Plan a visit during April to enjoy the French Camp Rodeo or to participate in the Mid-South Stargaze and Astronomy Conference. French Camp hosts an annual Harvest Festival in October.

GRENADA LAKE MUSEUM
2151 SCENIC LOOP 333
GRENADA, MS 38901

Snuggled inside the Grenada Lake Visitor Center, the Grenada Lake Museum focuses on Grenada's natural resources. The thirty-six-thousand-acre landscape surrounded by trees is home to Grenada Lake, filled with crappie, bass, bream and catfish. The two Confederate forts on the lake make this the perfect site for Civil War reenactors and presentations. Taxidermized wildlife provides a glimpse of what roams throughout the area. The visitor center offers information on the pristine camping facilities.

Gumtree Museum of Art
211 Main Street
Tupelo, MS 38804

The Gumtree Museum of Art celebrates fine art and artists with a mission to develop a high standard of visual art appreciation in Tupelo and surrounding areas. Walking into the old bank interior is like traveling back in time. Behind the vast vault door on the lobby floor, the former security room now serves as

*This page and opposite*: Gumtree Museum of Art. *Courtesy of Sondra Lee Bell.*

a supply space. The museum hosts exhibitions, solo shows, art organization and student shows, lectures, workshops and children's summer camps. The museum's influential partnership with the Gumtree Festival provides the community with a place welcoming both novice and master artists.

HEALTHWORKS!
A CHILDREN'S MUSEUM
219 SOUTH INDUSTRIAL ROAD
TUPELO, MS 38801

Affiliated with the North Mississippi Medical Center, HealthWorks! serves North Mississippi, Northwest Alabama and Southwest Tennessee. Its mission is "Infectiously contaminating kids of all ages, everywhere, to learn, have fun and make great choices by inspiring their passion and courage to lead healthy lives" and to provide educational services to the community and schools that encourage wellness choices.

## Historical Museum / Coca-Cola Display
223 First Street
Grenada, MS 38901

Welcome to Grenada, the "City That Smiles." Here, the museum lives in the heart of the city in the old Grenada Bank building, where exhibit collections reflect the city's history and Coca-Cola memorabilia, like banners, signs, posters, bottles, refrigerators and vending machines from earlier days. This museum houses one of the largest selections of Coca-Cola collectibles, second only to the museum in Atlanta, Georgia.

## Howlin' Wolf Museum
640 Commerce Street
West Point, MS 39773

Also known as the Black Prairie Blues Museum, the museum celebrates the legacy of Howlin' Wolf and other rhythm and blues artists. Inside are photos, replicas of albums, posters, guitars, cigar box guitars, awards, a wooden rooster, an old record player, articles of clothing, hats, artists' renderings and other memorabilia. A Howlin' Wolf Blues Festival takes place each year, and aside from hosting recognized blues performers, the museum also sponsors a component that educates the public on the blues.

## John Grisham Room
Mississippi State University
Mitchell Memorial Library, third floor
395 Hardy Road
Mississippi State (Starkville), MS 39759

In the late 1980s, MSU graduate John Grisham started donating some of his literary papers, along with personal correspondence, book-related promotions and newspaper and magazine clippings, the breadth of which spans his illustrious career. Opening in 1988, the John Grisham Room, a literary museum of sorts, includes files from Grisham's days in the legislature, correspondence to constituents and colleagues, manuscripts, screenplays and recordings.

## KEMPER COUNTY HISTORICAL MUSEUM
230 VETERANS STREET
DEKALB, MS 39328

Since 1986, the Kemper County Historical Museum in the old S.D. Mercantile Warehouse has displayed artifacts and memorabilia highlighting DeKalb and Kemper County's history. The warehouse, once a mercantile store selling feed, fertilizer and grain, now fills its brick walls with photos and posters. It also has an old safe, a phonograph, farm implements, historical articles and pictures of Kemper County families, some dating back to the 1800s. One display reflects the life of John Stennis, one of the longest-serving senators in Mississippi (1947–89) and a Mississippi House representative (1928–32). Kemper County was labeled "Bloody Kemper" after the Civil War due to fights, political squabbles and the murders of poor Black people by a local doctor involved in insurance fraud. DeKalb celebrates its Annual Heritage Day in October.

## KOSCIUSKO MUSEUM AND VISITORS CENTER
NATCHEZ TRACE PARKWAY, MILE MARKER 159.9
KOSCIUSKO, MS 39090

On the Natchez Trace, the Visitors Center's museum section provides information on Tadeusz Kościuszko, a Polish freedom fighter. His military and engineering skills played a vital role in the American Revolutionary War. The city of Kosciusko is named in his honor. The museum also includes information on Attala County and its iconic artisans and celebrities.

## KOSSUTH MUSEUM
35 CR 512
CORINTH, MS 38834

Located in a century-old post office, this museum exhibits local artifacts and references to the Corinth community.

LAKE HILL MOTORS MUSEUM
2003 HIGHWAY 72 EAST
CORINTH, MS 38834

The Lake Hill Motors dealership in Corinth also offers a vintage motorcycle museum filled with over 150 antique motorbikes and motorcycles of every shape and size, many restored to working condition. The museum opened in 2004 and is part of the Transamerica Trail (East Loop and West Loop), which maps out a scenic tour through Holly Springs National Forest to Batesville, Mississippi. Lake Hill Motors dealership has celebrated more than fifty years in business.

MANN-EAST-FRIDAY HOUSE MUSEUM
307 EAST WESTBROOK STREET
WEST POINT, MS 39773

The Mann-East-Friday House, built by Jabez Mann, a railroad machinist, in 1866, sits between the Court Street Historic District and the West Point Central City Historic District. Also referred to as the Friday House, the museum bears Mann's name, as well as his granddaughter's, Mrs. C.R. Friday. The museum exhibits the Payne Field, a World War I airfield located less than five miles outside of West Point. Named after Captain Dewitt Jennings Payne, it served as a military training base for pilots. The museum also highlights the history of West Point. Here you also find the Chester Arthur "Howlin' Wolf" Burnett Blues Museum, honoring Howlin' Wolf (1910–1976), a trailblazing entertainer and musician known for singing in his trademark gravelly voice and his howling like a wolf.

MARY BUIE MUSEUM
UNIVERSITY OF MISSISSIPPI
UNIVERSITY AVENUE AND SOUTH FIFTH STREET
OXFORD, MS 38655

Managed by the University of Mississippi, the Mary Buie Museum, founded in 1939, is named after artist Mary Skipwith Buie of Oxford and is the abode for her art collection. After Mary left the collection to the City of Oxford, her sister Kate Skipwith oversaw her vision with the help of family funding and government programs like the Works Progress Administration, which built the facility. Originally called the Oxford Art Center, the museum was renamed in 1942. Museum collections include various miniatures Buie painted when employed at Marshall Fields and her renditions of the Mona Lisa and Jean-Jacques Henner's *Penitent Magdalene*. Items from Kate Skipwith's collection of antiques, art, historic memorabilia, historic costumes, Civil War relics, dolls, fans and decorative art are also on display.

MISSISSIPPI ENTOMOLOGICAL MUSEUM
MISSISSIPPI STATE UNIVERSITY
100 OLD HIGHWAY 12
MISSISSIPPI STATE (STARKVILLE), MS 39762

The Mississippi Entomological Museum supports scientific research studying plants and insects and often conducts workshops on bugs, ants and plants. With 1.6 million specimens of insects, the museum's central purpose is documenting the biodiversity of the insect fauna. Eighteen researchers oversee the private and institutional collections representative of the state. The Mississippi Entomological Museum initiated the Mississippi Arthropod Survey in 1982 and the Midsouth Arthropod Survey in 1990, with the latter emphasizing arthropods in unique and threatened habitats in Mississippi, Alabama and Louisiana. An outreach program is the Mississippi Bug Blues Program.

NOXUBEE COUNTY HISTORICAL SOCIETY MUSEUM
JEFFERSON STREET AT COURTHOUSE SQUARE
MACON, MS 39341

The Noxubee County Historical Society was established in 1967. Its mission is to gather, preserve and share the history of Noxubee County, which covers Brooksville, Shuqualak and Macon (the county seat). Noxubee, once a part of the Choctaw Nation, is one of the state's oldest counties. Much of its history relates to the relinquishing of Native land. The museum, on the courthouse square, exhibits Noxubee County history, which encompasses the Choctaw Indians, African Americans and the Civil War. The Noxubee Historical Society also has records like the 1840 census listing the names of the county's slaveholders and the number of enslaved persons they owned.

OKTIBBEHA COUNTY HERITAGE MUSEUM
206 FELLOWSHIP STREET
STARKVILLE, MS 39759

The Oktibbeha County Heritage Museum celebrates the history of the county and its communities: Longview, Mississippi State, Starkville and Sturgis. Oktibbeha is the Choctaw word for "icy waters." Established in 1976, the museum is in the renovated 1874 Mobile & Ohio Railroad Depot. Antiques and artifacts include an 1840 square piano; Native American and Civil War artifacts; military memorabilia; items related to aviation history, including that of female aviation pioneer Lynn Spruill, photographs and other mementos; a retro doctor's office; the history of the local Coca-Cola Company; Rockwood pottery; the Herschede Hall Clock; donated items from a local shoe shop and shoeshine parlor; information on agriculture in the area (such as dairy farming and forestry); and a miniature railroad layout. A sports display highlights notables, such as baseball player "Cool Papa" Bell, NBA star Bailey Howell and NFL standout Jerry Rice.

OLD TISHOMINGO COUNTY COURTHOUSE AND MUSEUM
203 EAST QUITMAN STREET
IUKA, MS 38852

The Old Tishomingo County Courthouse and Museum is a nineteenth-century restored Romanesque building of the Second Empire. It is listed in the National Register of Historic Places. The Tishomingo County Historical and Genealogical Society also makes its home there, as does the John Marshall Stone Research Library. Celebrating the history of Iuka, Burnsville, Belmont and Golden, the museum displays artifacts related to Chickasaw Indians, the Civil War and cultural heritage; old court documents; memorabilia; county archives; antiques; and more. Tishomingo County is known for its historic homes, cemeteries, old buildings and the Battle of Iuka and other Civil War events.

OREN DUNN CITY MUSEUM
689 RUTHERFORD ROAD
TUPELO, MS 38801

Named after its founder, Oren F. Dunn, the Oren Dunn City Museum collects and preserves the history of Tupelo, Lee County and Northeast Mississippi. Through its diverse collection of Native American fossils, the museum tells the story of the Chickasaw living near the Tombigbee River headwaters and throughout the Mississippi River valley and the stories of Tupelo, the Natchez Trace Parkway, the 1936 Tupelo Tornado and the Hospital on the Hill. Other displays celebrate musicians from the Tupelo community, such as the Velvelettes and Mississippi Slim, and folklife through antique farm equipment, sewing machines, clothing and a printing press. Children love to see the model train with community landscaping representing the city of Tupelo. Visitors will want to explore the museum grounds, where they will find the Lee County Book Mobile, the first in the region to serve African Americans (1939–65), a nineteenth-century blacksmith shop, a sorghum mill, an old Frisco Railroad caboose and Spark's church and school buildings,

Oren Dunn City Museum. *Courtesy of Sondra Lee Bell.*

*This page and opposite*: Oren Dunn City Museum. *Courtesy of Sondra Lee Bell.*

**The Velvelettes**

The two founding members of The Velvelettes were Mildred Gill and Bertha Barbee. Barbee grew up in Shannon. She got her cousin, Norma Barbee, also of Shannon to join the group.

The girls biggest song in the United States was "Needle in A Haystack" which peaked at number 45 on the Billboard Hot 100 in 1964.

For more, search out a Turquoise Binder.

which were moved to the museum location. The facilities provide a glimpse into the past, and an 1870s dogtrot house was donated to the museum in 1984. The early twentieth-century Memphis streetcar brought to Tupelo in 1947 was converted into Dudie's Diner, known for its breakfast menu, barbecue and Dudie Burgers. Don't forget to visit the gift shop!

RAILS AND TRAILS MUSEUM
100 TRUMAN STREET
BOONEVILLE, MS 38829

In 2009, the Prentiss County Genealogical and Historical Society established the Rails and Trails Museum inside the historic Gulf, Mobile & Ohio Depot. Built around 1890 (the original depot was burned down during the Civil War), the depot sits in the Downtown Booneville Historic District and is listed in the National Register of Historic Places. As a museum, the vintage building stores artifacts, weapons, uniforms and other memorabilia from the Civil War Battle of Booneville, a Magnolia Flag, knives, guns, an 1865 Colt revolver and military trophies from World War II and the Korean and Vietnam Wars. The museum is made even more intriguing with wagons, buggies, old newspaper articles and photos from the 1950s and '60s. There is also a collection of artifacts from the area's Native American population, a seventy-million-year-old fossil, shark teeth, turtle shells and crocodile plates. On the same property is the only room left of the Cunningham House, an antebellum home moved from its original location on the Booneville First Baptist Church property.

R.E. HUNT MUSEUM & CULTURAL CENTER
924 TWENTIETH STREET NORTH
COLUMBUS, MS 39703

The R.E. Hunt Museum & Cultural Center opened in 2011 and is located at the old Hunt High School in the former Fine Arts Building. The high school opened in 1954 and closed in 1971, due in part to desegregation. The community wanted to continue encouraging students and others by creating a museum to celebrate (against all obstacles) the school's achievements and its students. The museum is dedicated to collecting, preserving, interpreting and celebrating the history and heritage of African

Americans in Columbus and Lowndes County. Artifacts, pictures, articles and other materials exhibit how the oppressed Black population surpassed the expected outcome of their people. Museum items showcase teachers, students, businesses and professionals who were amazing trailblazers. The museum celebrates the school's football, basketball and baseball teams, as well as the school band. Today, the old Hunt High School building is a Mississippi Historic Landmark.

SAM WILHITE TRANSPORTATION MUSEUM
210 DEPOT DRIVE
WEST POINT, MS 39773

The old Illinois Central Railroad Depot, constructed in 1894, houses the Sam Wilhite Transportation Museum and its exhibits of railroad artifacts, memorabilia, pictures and information from Sam Wilhite's personal collection. The exhibits relate to past transportation in West Point and reflect on the Native American trails and transportation initiatives dating back two hundred years and continuing to modern-day highways. The walls contain pictures of various modes of historical transportation. A 1927 Model T Ford, once the Columbus & Greenville Railroad's inspection car, lives at the museum. A museum area set up as a train station with the original ticket window has wax mannequins dressed in period clothing. The large-scale model train station with an HO-scale railroad represents the three Golden Triangle towns and includes MSU's football stadium in Starkville, Golden Triangle Airport in Columbus, the 1872 Henley House in West Point, a livestock company, a plantation and more.

TENNESSEE WILLIAMS HOUSE & WELCOME CENTER MUSEUM
300 MAIN STREET
COLUMBUS, MS 39701

The Tennessee Williams House is a restored 1875 Victorian home that was once the rectory of St. Paul's Episcopal Church before it was moved to its current location. The house later became the Columbus Welcome Center and a National Literary Landmark. Author Thomas Lanier "Tennessee" Williams III was born in this house and lived there for three years. His grandfather Reverend Walter Edwin Dakin was the St. George's Episcopal

Tennessee Williams House & Welcome Center Museum. *Courtesy of Richelle Putnam.*

Church rector in Clarksdale, Mississippi, and Tennessee lived with him for a while, forming some of his earliest memories in Clarksdale. Tennessee died in New York City in 1983. Columbus hosts an annual Stella Shouting Contest honoring a line from the 1951 movie adaptation of the 1947 Pulitzer Prize–winning three-act Broadway play *A Streetcar Named Desire*, written by Williams. The line mimics Marlon Brando's famous blood-curdling shout in the movie. The annual Tennessee Williams Tribute and contest takes place in September.

TIPPAH COUNTY HISTORICAL MUSEUM
106 SIDDALL STREET
RIPLEY, MS 38663

The Tippah County Historical Museum inside the Tippah County Courthouse preserves historical information about the county's past and its journey into the future. The 1870 building is the third to be erected; the first was a log cabin, and the second burned in 1861 during the Civil War. Displays include photographs, paintings, rare fossils, memorabilia, artifacts such as spinning wheels and looms, period clothing and articles related to

World Wars I and II and the Civil War. An enlarged map lists the names of early Tippah settlers, and there are references to legends who once lived in the area, like John Grisham, opera and movie star Ruby Elzy, "Father of Bluegrass" Bill Monroe, William Faulkner and the infamous Colonel William Falkner, great-grandfather of the author, who feuded with friend and business partner R.J. Thurmond. The outcome left Falkner dead on the streets of Ripley.

TOWN SQUARE POST OFFICE AND MUSEUM
59 SOUTH MAIN STREET
PONTOTOC, MS 38863

Established in 1998 and operated by the Pontotoc County Historical Society, the Town Square Post Office and Museum celebrates bygone folklife and reflects on Chickasaw Native Americans, pioneers and early explorers in the Pontotoc area. The lobby mural of the 1540 explorer Hernando de Soto and three Chickasaw chiefs' meeting prepares visitors for their journey through the museum, with exhibits highlighting the railroad, veterans, education and early home and community life through documents, books, photographs, memorabilia, artifacts, local traditions, artistry and exhibits representing businesses like the E.H. Carter General Stores and the Elizabeth Ann Barr's millinery and dress shop, which operated from 1861 to 1929. A model of Dr. John Patterson's office is also on display. The gift shop offers books, collectibles, postcards, T-shirts and more.

TUPELO VETERANS MUSEUM
689 RUTHERFORD ROAD
TUPELO, MS 38801

The Tupelo Veterans Museum offers an in-depth collection of memorabilia. United States Army veteran Tony Lutes, the owner and curator of the museum, graciously shared his sixty years of treasured finds. Exhibits include Civil War memorabilia, including guns, swords, uniforms, maps, pictures, artifacts and a signed document by Abraham Lincoln. Displays of World Wars I and II include a jeep, weapons, uniforms, books, photos, movies and a large collection of airplane and ship models. The Korean, Vietnam and Gulf Wars are also represented with radios, field telephones,

This page and opposite:
Tupelo Veterans
Museum. *Courtesy of
Sondra Lee Bell.*

guns, uniforms, maps, flight suits and field equipment. Other displays highlight a Nazi banner, a Seiko working clock from a crashed Japanese Zero, a German Luger, a .32-caliber officer's dress pistol, a 9mm German Radom and other items.

Ulysses S. Grant Presidential Library Museum
Mississippi State University
Mitchell Memorial Library, fourth floor
395 Hardy Road
Mississippi State (Starkville), MS 39759

The Ulysses S. Grant Presidential Library Museum on the fourth floor of the Mitchell Memorial Library on the campus of Mississippi State University in Starkville presents Grant's life as a military cadet, general, president of the United States and elder statesperson. Grant made an impressive stance in Mississippi during the Civil War and is remembered for his role in leading the Union army's siege of Vicksburg. Exhibits include artifacts, sculptures, life-size statues of Grant, films, interactive media screens, autographed manuscripts and a portrait of Grant that once hung in the National Portrait Gallery. The interactive media layout has a map of Grant's funeral procession route as it moved through the streets of New York, with portraits of Grant's family and of Grant himself.

Union County Historical Society and Heritage Museum
114 Cleveland Street
New Albany, MS 38652

The Union County Historical Society and Heritage Museum, initially housed in a church, is in downtown New Albany and encompasses more than a city block. The museum, with eleven thousand square feet of space, includes a library, gift shop and six galleries with permanent exhibits and expressions of life, culture and county commerce. The literary garden celebrates the life of William Faulkner, born just one block away. Outside, visitors find the Storyteller's Chair, Varner's Country Store, a caboose, an early twentieth-century doctor's office, a blacksmith shop, a 1950 autobody shop, an agricultural exhibit and folk art. The Barn Quilt Trail includes more than one hundred quilts, and the Hallelujah Trail celebrates the county's century-old churches, many of which are historic African American churches. The museum has also gathered information on the pre–civil rights history of the African American business district and has sponsored two Mississippi Blues Trail markers and five historic markers.

THE UNIVERSITY OF MISSISSIPPI MUSEUM
UNIVERSITY AVENUE AND SOUTH FIFTH STREET
OXFORD, MS 38655

The University of Mississippi Museum collection includes the Millington-Bernard Collection of Scientific Instruments from the nineteenth century (1848–61), telescopes, models of large machines and demonstration devices for teaching natural philosophy, physics and astronomy. It also houses the David M. Robinson Collection of Greek and Roman Antiquities, which covers the period 1500 BCE to CE 300. Other displays include sculptures, pottery, ceramic artifacts and coins. The Seymour Lawrence Collection of American Art was donated by publisher Seymour Lawrence and includes works by notables such as Georgia O'Keeffe and Kurt Vonnegut. The Theora Hamblett Collection is a folk-art collection of over two hundred works of art. The University of Mississippi manages Rowan Oak, William Faulkner's home; the Mary Buie Museum; and the Walton-Young Historic House.

Mississippi Museum of Art. *Courtesy of Richelle Putnam.*

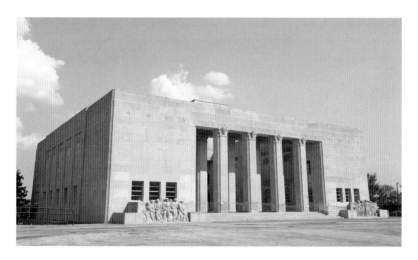

Mississippi War Museum. *Courtesy of Richelle Putnam.*

Part III

# CENTRAL MISSISSIPPI

BIEDENHARN COCA-COLA MUSEUM
1107 WASHINGTON STREET
VICKSBURG, MS 39183

The Biedenharn Coca-Cola Museum in downtown Vicksburg focuses on a family soda fountain business that became the first to bottle Coca-Cola. The Biedenharn bottling operation lasted until 1938. The building ended up with several different owners, but in 1979, the Biedenharn family repurchased and restored the building and donated it to the Vicksburg Foundation for Historic Preservation. Through artifacts and memorabilia, the Biedenharn Coca-Cola Museum shares the history of the family, the original bottling process and information about the soft drink. There is a marble soda fountain from the early 1900s and Coca-Cola bottles with the Biedenharn name embossed on them. The fountains traditionally held other flavors, such as grape, peach, sarsaparilla and peppermint, and visitors can still enjoy ice cream, fountain cokes, coke floats and more. The candy store is replicated to look as it did in the 1890s and offers treats like old-fashioned candy sticks, rock candy and gummy bears.

Canton Convention and Visitors Bureau
Canton (Film) Movie Museum
Canton Multi-Cultural Museum
Canton History Museum
Canton Depot Museum
Old Madison County Jail Museum
147 North Union Street
Canton, MS 39046

The Canton Movie Museum, also known as the My Dog Skip Museum (named after the movie of the same name that was based on the book by Mississippi author Willie Morris), is a place of remembrance because of all the movies that have been filmed in the city. The producers of movies such as *A Time to Kill*, *My Dog Skip*, *O Brother, Where Art Thou?*, *The Rising Place* and *A Ponder Heart* found the town to be a good backdrop. There is a lot to see in this museum, including artifacts from movies filmed in Canton.

The Canton Multi-Cultural Museum allows visitors to discover stories of Madison County, its families, businesses and community, with a focus on the civil rights era.

The 1890 depot housing the Canton Depot Museum was purchased by the Canton Redevelopment Authority, and restorations were completed in 1999. The museum reflects on Madison County and the railroad history of Canton, including a train stop of the famed Casey Jones, who died in 1900 trying to save his passengers' lives.

Located in the old jail, the Canton History Museum includes artifacts of merchants and businesses from the early 1800s, such as a butter churn, a bank teller adding machine, a pharmacist's medicine counter and an old-fashioned coke machine cooler.

The Old Madison County Jail Museum is located in a former jail. Built in 1870, the jail closed in 1969 and is listed in the National Register of Historic Places. The design of the building is reminiscent of Civil War architecture, and on the grounds is a historic log cabin dating to 1777.

Catfish Row Museum
913 Washington Street
Vicksburg, MS 39180

The Catfish Row Museum is in the Christian and Brough Building, erected in 1905 as a manufacturing site for blacksmithing. It later became a dealership selling Packard and Studebaker automobiles, and in the 1970s and '80s it was a blues club presenting national touring acts. The museum opened in 2021 to provide opportunities for learning Vicksburg's history and culture. Exhibits relate to the river and the people who settled in the area, the folklife of Vicksburg natives dating to the 1800s, information about Warren County and Vicksburg's military history. The museum highlights cultural influences on the area, like the Mississippi Delta and diverse ethnic groups such as African Americans, Jews, Italians, Greeks, Lebanese and Chinese. On-site technology allows visitors to scan photos, letters, recipes and more, which is a great opportunity to contribute to the museum's research. The museum's oral history project includes plans to record interviews to gain assorted perspectives on the city's illustrious history. The museum presents live performances, panel discussions, lectures, special events, programs and hands-on workshops.

CHAHTA IMMI CULTURAL CENTER
101 INDUSTRIAL DRIVE
MERIDIAN, MS 39350

When the Choctaw Museum closed, the Chahta Immi Cultural Center in the Choctaw Town Center took over the responsibility of celebrating the history of the Choctaw Tribal Nation and the Mississippi Band of Choctaw Indians. As European settlers immigrated to America, the Choctaw Nation already occupied the southern states. Today, there are close to ten thousand members of the Mississippi Band of Choctaw Indians living in communities throughout the state. The museum exhibits the life of Choctaw Native Americans through displays of art, archival collections, educational programming, classes and events. One of the goals of the center is to preserve the Choctaw language. Events taking place at the center include storytelling by tribal elders.

CRAFTSMEN'S GUILD OF MISSISSIPPI
WILLIAM L. "BILL" WALLER CRAFTS CENTER
950 RICE ROAD
RIDGELAND, MS 39157

Founded in 1973, the Craftsmen's Guild of Mississippi was created to promote and preserve traditional, folk and contemporary crafts. It previously occupied

Craftsmen's Guild of Mississippi, William L. "Bill" Waller Crafts Center. *Courtesy of the Craftsmen's Guild.*

COME SEE MISSISSIPPI'S

*Snappy Sync Fireflies*

Experience the magic of synchronous "snappy sync" fireflies along the historic Natchez Trace

**WALLER CRAFT CENTER**

Craftsmen's Guild of Mississippi, William L. "Bill" Waller Crafts Center. *Courtesy of the Craftsmen's Guild.*

two facilities: (1) a dogtrot cabin on the historic Natchez Trace Parkway, and (2) a section of the Mississippi Agricultural and Forestry Museum in Jackson. The center was moved to its current location and renamed to honor William Lowe Waller Sr. (1926–2011), Mississippi's fifty-sixth governor. Waller, an attorney from Oxford, understood the importance of education and arts and crafts. The center was launched during his administration. The guild maintains the highest standard of excellence and sells only the finest crafts designed by skilled guild members and such notables as woodcarver George Berry. The collection incorporates an impressive medley of Native American basketry, pottery, weaving and jewelry. Every three years, each craft member's work is adjudicated until they attain a "fellow" status to indicate a mastery level of quality workmanship. On-site demonstrations and classes take place throughout the year. Exhibits in the gallery include works created in wood, fabric, metal, glass, fibers, pottery and more. In December, the guild hosts the popular event Chimneyville. Another event is Sheep to Shawl, which demonstrates the shearing, carding and spinning of wool. A popular annual tourist attraction is the Snappy Sync firefly event in May behind the center on the Natchez Trace.

INTERNATIONAL MUSEUM OF MUSLIM CULTURES
201 EAST PASCAGOULA STREET
JACKSON, MS 39201

An interactive interpretive center, the International Museum of Muslim Cultures has continued to be an invaluable resource and education center with permanent historic gallery exhibits, as well as installations celebrating the legacy of Muslims and Islam. A notable traveling exhibition was *Spirit of Ramadan*, which celebrated the Islamic holy time when Muslims around the world renew their focus on their spiritual life. This rededication is a time of fasting, prayer, reflection, abstinence and community. Other exhibitions include *Muslims with Christians and Jews: An Exhibition of Covenant and Co-existence*, *Legacy of Timbuktu: Wonders of the Written Word* and *Moorish Spain: Its Legacy to Europe and the West*.

JACKSON FIRE MUSEUM
355 WEST WOODROW WILSON AVENUE
JACKSON, MS 39213

Also known as Jackson's Public Fire Safety Education Center, the Jackson Fire Museum is housed inside the No. 10 fire station and serves as an active firehouse. The museum includes Jackson's early fire trucks, a 1904 Nott horse-drawn steam engine and a 1917 chain-driven American LaFrance. Other exhibits are an 1870 parade uniform, communications equipment, helmets, a 1936 Seagrave truck and historical records. In addition, there are toy replicas, a trampoline, artifacts and fire apparatus from the early 1800s. The museum also has a memorial to 9/11 and local crew members who have lost their lives in the line of duty. The museum's purpose is to educate the public on the history of the Jackson Fire Department.

JESSE BRENT LOWER MISSISSIPPI RIVER MUSEUM
910 WASHINGTON STREET
VICKSBURG, MS 39180

The Jesse Brent Lower Mississippi River Museum, in downtown Vicksburg along the Yazoo River, is managed by the Army Corp of Engineers–Vicksburg District. Its purpose is to educate and engage what the Mississippi

River means to the surrounding communities. Incorporated into the exhibits are a fish aquarium (1,515 gallons), towboat, vessel and information displays, as well as a 1927 flood wall and tent. Visitors can explore the *M/V Mississippi IV* vessel on a self-guided tour using the ship's "tour cards."

## Jimmie Rodgers Museum
## 1200 Twenty-Second Avenue
## Meridian, MS 39301

The Jimmie Rodgers Museum reveals the life of the singer and the legacy of his career. Exhibits include the original guitar of the "Singing Brakeman" and other memorabilia from his life, as well as railroad equipment from the era of steam-engine travel. Born in Lauderdale County on September 8, 1897, Jimmie Rodgers was thirteen when he got his first job as a water boy on his father's railroad gang. Between 1927, when Rodgers auditioned for Ralph Peer, a Victor Talking Machine Company representative in Bristol, Tennessee, and Rodgers's death in 1933, he recorded more than one hundred songs and sold about twelve million records. Considered the "Father of Country Music," Rodgers was one of the first artists inducted into the Country Music Hall of Fame. He was inducted into the Rock & Roll Hall of Fame and the Nashville Songwriters Hall of Fame. He received the first Mississippi Country Music Trail marker and was honored with a Mississippi Blues Trail marker. He cowrote with his sister-in-law Elsie McWilliams, who was inducted into the Nashville Songwriters Hall of Fame.

## Key Brothers Aviation Museum
## Meridian Regional Airport
## 2811 Airport Boulevard
## Meridian, MS 39307

The Key Brothers Aviation Museum at the Key Field airport terminal building was dedicated in November 1977. The administration building and hangar are in the National Register of Historic Places as early aviation structures for their involvement in the Key brothers' world flight endurance record. Exhibits include photos of Al and Fred Key and their flights and a model replica of the Ole Miss five-cylinder "Wright Whirlwind" engine. During the Great Depression, to attract attention and notoriety for the

Jimmie Rodgers Museum. *Courtesy of Richelle Putnam.*

Key Brothers Museum. *Courtesy of Richelle Putnam.*

struggling Meridian Municipal Airport, Fred and Al planned a flight over Meridian to break the 553-hour world endurance record held by the Hunter brothers of Chicago. On June 4, 1935, the Key brothers set a world record in a Curtis Robin aircraft, the *Ole Miss.* It ended twenty-seven days later, on July 1, 1935, after Fred and Al Key had flown 52,320 miles nonstop and landed at Meridian Regional Airport, where a crowd of thirty thousand cheered their landing.

LAUDERDALE COUNTY DEPARTMENT OF ARCHIVES AND HISTORY
500 CONSTITUTION AVENUE
MERIDIAN, MS 39301

Currently, the Lauderdale County Department of Archives and History is packing its archival material on the second floor of the courthouse annex building for a move across the street to the historic Lauderdale County Courthouse. Constructed in 1905 under the direction of Meridian architects Penn J. Krouse and C.L. Hutchisson, the Mississippi Landmark courthouse was remodeled during the Great Depression by the same architects. It is listed in the National Register of Historic Places as contributing element no. 123 in the Downtown Meridian Historic District.

Lauderdale County Department of Archives and History. *Courtesy of Richelle Putnam.*

Lauderdale County Department of Archives and History. *Courtesy of Richelle Putnam.*

The Lauderdale County Department of Archives and History, the first county archives department organized in the state, manages county records and documents and holds a wealth of historical information. Displays include photos, signs, arrowheads, military items and more. Civil War buffs enjoy a work of more than forty volumes on Civil War soldiers titled *Confederate Deaths & Burials*. The archives also house *The Civil War Diary*, both written by James Palmer. Archives employees and volunteers are involved in ongoing research projects, which are published in-house and placed for sale in the archives bookstore.

MARIE HULL GALLERY
HINDS COMMUNITY COLLEGE
1310 SEVEN SPRINGS DRIVE
RAYMOND, MS 39154

The Marie Hull Gallery (also known as the Art Department Gallery) hosts six exhibitions of local and regional artists' works between October and May each year on the campus of Hinds Community College in the Katherine Denton Art Building. Marie Atkinson Hull (1890–1980) was a prolific artist known for portraits, landscape paintings, illustrations, printmaking and sculpture.

MARTY STUART'S CONGRESS OF COUNTRY MUSIC
311 BYRD AVENUE
PHILADELPHIA, MS 39350

The Congress of Country Music, scheduled to open with Phase 1 in December 2023, "will celebrate the rich cultural heritage of country music through live musical performances, educational programs and a world-class country music museum and performing arts center." Philadelphia native and five-time GRAMMY winner Marty Stuart has collected over twenty thousand items to tell a rich, emotional and personal story of the lives to be celebrated in his hometown. The recently renovated Ellis Theater hosted sell-out shows, including a Dolly Parton fundraising effort for the center, a $30 million, fifty-thousand-plus-square-foot project. In addition to the historic Ellis Theater, there will be a newly constructed museum, classrooms, community hall, meeting and event space and a rooftop performance venue. Revolving exhibits of internationally traveled artifacts and memorabilia, photography, outsider/folk art and Native American crafts will all embrace the roots of country music.

Meridian Museum of Art
628 Twenty-Fifth Avenue
Meridian, MS 39301

The Meridian Museum of Art (MMA) is housed in the historic Old Carnegie Library building constructed about 1912–13, which is listed in the National Register of Historic Places and is a Mississippi Landmark. The museum promotes and supports local and regional art and artists and hosts many programs through art education, exhibitions, collections, collaborations with other organizations, special events and community involvement. Exhibits feature the finest artists in Mississippi and Alabama in solo and group shows, invitational exhibits and the Bi-State Competition.

Meridian Railroad Museum
AMTRAK Station
1805 Front Street
Meridian, MS 39301

Housed in the more than one-hundred-year-old restored Railway Express Agency building, the Meridian Railroad Museum tells the stories of the city's railroads through photographs, artifacts and a model railroad. The Mobile & Ohio (M&O) Railroad, one of the country's earliest land grant railroads, was the first rail line built into Lauderdale County in 1855, and in October, the first train arrived at "McLemore Field," years before Meridian became incorporated as a town. On May 29, 1861, the first Southern Railway of Mississippi train, led by the *Mazeppa* engine, crossed the M&O tracks and arrived in Meridian at 6:56 p.m. The Selma & Meridian Railroad was completed on December 10, 1862, the New Orleans & Northeastern line on November 14, 1883 and the Meridian & Bigbee River Railway on April 15, 1928. Outside the museum, the first two markers on Meridian's Civil War Trail highlight the importance of railroads during the war. The museum hosts Railfest each November.

*Top*: Meridian Museum of Art. *Courtesy of Richelle Putnam*. *Bottom*: Meridian Railroad Museum. *Courtesy of Richelle Putnam*.

MISSISSIPPI AGRICULTURE AND FORESTRY MUSEUM
1150 LAKELAND DRIVE
JACKSON, MS 39216

The museum's goal is "to cultivate an appreciation for Mississippi agriculture and create a memorable experience that inspires the community as a whole," with a mission "to create an environment that communicates the value of past and present Mississippi agricultural lifestyles, relationships and practices and their relevance to the future of all people." It is the perfect venue for school field trips, and visitors enjoy the Forestry and Sparkman buildings, Ethnic Heritage Center, Education Center, Masonic Lodge, multipurpose center, Bisland cotton gin, quaint church building, general store, historical farmstead, forest study trail, children's barnyard and the National Agricultural Aviation Museum. The extensive artifact collection and lifelike exhibits (dioramas) include a living history farm, crossroads town, forest study area, train exhibit, nature trail, the Fitzgerald artifact collection, Fortenberry-Parkman Farm restoration and flower and vegetable gardens.

MISSISSIPPI ARTS + ENTERTAINMENT EXPERIENCE (THE MAX)
2155 FRONT STREET
MERIDIAN, MS 39301

The Mississippi Arts + Entertainment Experience (The MAX) showcases Mississippi's legacy in every art distinction, honoring legends in the arts and entertainment fields. The center seeks to inspire tomorrow's artists through exhibitions, performances, classes and events. Permanent exhibits include *Feel the Land*, *Go Back Home*, *Share Community*, *The Power of the Church*, *Explore Who and Where* and *Reach Out to the World*. The Hall of Fame recognizes such Mississippi icons as Elvis Presley, B.B. King, Eudora Welty, William Faulkner, Margaret Walker Alexander, Tennessee Williams, Sam Cooke, W.C. Handy, Ida B. Wells, Alice Walker, Morgan Freeman, Jim Henson and more. The center hosts tours, various artist and industry workshops and special events while also guiding visitors to other Mississippi towns and museums, from Elvis Presley's Tupelo and B.B. King's Indianola, to Jimmy Buffett's Pascagoula, Eudora Welty's Jackson and Walter Anderson's Ocean Springs. The state-of-the-art recording studio contains the latest technology for live recording, tracking and session work, podcasts, long-form audio recording for documentaries and audio beds for commercials.

## MISSISSIPPI CHILDREN'S MUSEUM, JACKSON
## 2145 MUSEUM BOULEVARD
## JACKSON, MS 39202

The hope of the Mississippi Children's Museum is "to create unparalleled experiences to inspire excellence and a lifelong joy of learning" with a vision to "inspire Mississippi's children from all backgrounds to discover and achieve their potential." To do so, the museum created hands-on learning in the arts and sciences with classrooms and 9,500 square feet of indoor exhibition space that also houses a 3D printer and robotics, a circle tree, building

activities and crafting materials. The Wonder Box Exhibits tells Mississippi's rich history of innovative creators. The museum hosts the nation's only Good Night Moon exhibit and participates in the Barksdale Reading Institute LIFT program (Learn, Inspire, Fulfill and Teach). In addition, twenty-thousand square feet of outdoor exhibit space includes an edible garden.

Mississippi Children's Museum, Jackson.
*Courtesy of Diane Williams.*

MISSISSIPPI CHILDREN'S MUSEUM, MERIDIAN
403 TWENTY-SECOND AVENUE
MERIDIAN, MS 39301

The Mississippi Children's Museum was born when a group of community volunteers realized the critical need to improve the health, literacy and well-being of the state's children. The mission of the museum is "to create unparalleled experiences to inspire excellence and a lifelong joy of learning." The museum does this through hands-on exhibits and programs focusing on literacy, STEAM (science, technology, engineering, art and math) and health and nutrition. Another focus is improving the early literacy development of Mississippi's children through place-based experiences containing literacy and language concepts and programs focusing on the mechanics and enjoyment of reading. New to the MCM-Meridian program is its after-school program for a limited number of K–5 children. MCM-Meridian hosts traveling exhibits and rents space for birthday parties and other special events.

*Top*: Mississippi Arts + Entertainment Museum. *Bottom*: Mississippi Children's Museum, Meridian. *Both, courtesy of Richelle Putnam.*

MISSISSIPPI INDUSTRIAL HERITAGE MUSEUM (SOULÉ STEAM FEED WORKS)
1808 FOURTH STREET
MERIDIAN, MS 39301

The museum displays the Soulé company's most noted products sold around the world. The factory building houses about 80 percent of its original furnishings and equipment and, therefore, still looks as it did from the 1920s through the 1940s. The last steam engine produced at the factory and a rare Soulé Rotary Steam Engine (patented 1896 and 1902) is displayed and operated in the steam demonstration room. George W. Soulé, the Meridian inventor and industrialist who held more than twenty-five U.S. patents, founded Soulé Steam Feed Works in 1892. The factory manufactured products for the booming lumber industry from 1885 until 1930. Its first invention and developed product, the Soulé Rotary Steam Engine, was used in sawmills to "feed the log and carriage through the sawblade," hence the term *steam feed*. Soulé invented the first automation used in sawmills, which included his automatic lumber stacker, which stacked lumber on carts that transported the lumber to dry kilns. Soulé produced about 2,300 Rotary Steam Engines and 4,301 Speed-Twin Steam Engines.

Mississippi Industrial Heritage Museum (Soulé Steam Feed Works). *Courtesy of Richelle Putnam.*

MISSISSIPPI MUSEUM OF ART
380 SOUTH LAMAR STREET
JACKSON, MS 39201

Founded in 1978, the Mississippi Museum of Art is the largest museum in Mississippi. Formerly known as the Mississippi Art Association established in 1911 for the purpose of exhibiting art, the museum's collections have grown to over 5,800 objects, with a strong focus on nineteenth- and twentieth-century American art by beloved artists such as Georgia O'Keeffe, Romare Bearden,

Andy Warhol, Sam Gilliam, Mary Lovelace O'Neal and Robert Henri. Other highlights include a permanent collection with over two hundred objects, world-class traveling exhibits and an outdoor art garden with Wi-Fi, where visitors can explore the seasonal foliage and performances on the outdoor stage. The museum produces humanities-based programming and activities to strengthen diversity, equity and inclusion and has a gift shop and café.

Mississippi Museum of Natural Science
2148 Riverside Drive
Jackson, MS 39201

With a mission "to promote understanding and appreciation of Mississippi's biological diversity through collections, research, scientific databases, education and exhibits; and to inspire the people of Mississippi to respect the environment and to preserve natural Mississippi," the Mississippi Museum of Natural Science evolved out of a love of nature. Started in 1932, accredited by the American Alliance of Museums and a member of the Association of Science-Technology Centers, the museum delivers hands-on learning. The venue includes a one-hundred-thousand-gallon aquarium with two hundred living species of fish, an amphitheater, two and a half miles of natural trails and 73,000 square feet of permanent and temporary exhibits, including deer, birds, alligators, waterfowl, snapping turtles, reptiles, mammals, invertebrates, plants, amphibians, fossils, a giant sloth and an endangered species exhibit.

Mississippi Music Experience at the Iron Horse Grill
320 West Pearl Street
Jackson, MS 39203

The Mississippi Music Experience, housed in the 1906 Armour Smokehouse in downtown Jackson, serves as "a tribute to the deep roots American music has in our state" and tells the stories of Mississippi, the "Birthplace of America's Music." The restaurant makes an impressive connection to music through live performances on the main stage. Exhibits include Anne Robin Luckett's lifelike wax statues of famous Mississippi musicians, memorabilia from 1800 to the current era, as well as timelines, records, pictures and signs, like the Dockery Farms sign.

## MISSISSIPPI PETRIFIED FOREST
124 FOREST PARK ROAD
FLORA, MS 39071

The Mississippi Petrified Forest is one of only two petrified forests in the eastern region of the United States; the other is Gilboa Fossil Forest in Schoharie County, New York. The Mississippi Petrified Forest was declared a National Natural Landmark in 1965. On-site is an Earth Science Center exhibiting petrified wood, plant life, fruits, cones, bark, fossil wood, dinosaur footprints, whale bones, turtle shells and a cast from a prehistoric camel.

## MISSISSIPPI SPORTS HALL OF FAME AND MUSEUM
1152 LAKELAND DRIVE
JACKSON, MS 39216

The Mississippi Sports Hall of Fame and Museum opened on July 4, 1996, with a mission "to preserve, protect, and promote Mississippi's rich sports heritage for this and future generations." Honoring athletes, coaches and influential sports icons in baseball, football, basketball, auto racing, boxing, golf, softball, tennis and track and field, the exhibits tell the story of resilience and a strong commitment to sports. Children five years of age and older enjoy hands-on experiences, like throwing a baseball, kicking a soccer ball, playing games and pretending to be a sportscaster in the broadcast booth. Memorabilia of the legendary Jay Hanna "Dizzy" Dean, a former St. Louis Cardinals pitcher, are displayed on the second floor. He is remembered for winning thirty games in 1934 and twenty-eight in 1935.

## MISSISSIPPI STATE HOSPITAL MUSEUM
3550 MS-468
PEARL, MS 39208

The Mississippi State Hospital, known now as Whitfield in honor of former governor Henry L. Whitfield and formerly known as the Mississippi State Lunatic Asylum and Mississippi State Insane Hospital, is a state facility treating mental health disorders. The University of Mississippi Medical Center in Jackson sits on the site where the original Mississippi State Lunatic Asylum was built in 1855 and renamed the State Hospital for the Insane in

Mississippi State Hospital Museum. *Courtesy of Diane Williams.*

1900. The museum opened in early 2000 in building no. 23 at the current location, which, prior to the mid-1960s, housed only white patients on the segregated campus. The museum's exhibitions reference the hospital's hydrotherapy rooms, needle spray showers and fever boxes, rendering an earnest perspective about the limited knowledge and understanding of treating mental disabilities in the past. For over thirty years, the hospital has hosted an art/auction show, Serendipity, showcasing the patients' artworks, paintings, drawings and sculptures. The famous Mississippi artist Walter Anderson, who was diagnosed with schizophrenia and depression, was a patient at the hospital. The museum's collection of works by Anderson includes artworks he created during his stay.

MUNICIPAL ART GALLERY OF JACKSON
839 NORTH STATE STREET
JACKSON, MS 39202

The Municipal Art Gallery of Jackson, in the former home of John and Sarah Ligon, exhibits the permanent art collection of works by Karl Wolfe, Mildred Wolfe, Andrew Bucci, William Hollingsworth and Marie Hull. The building, erected in the 1860s, is one of Jackson's oldest surviving historical structures and opened as a gallery museum in 1926. Containing three hundred square feet of wall space, two thousand square feet of floor space, a live performance space and an outdoor courtyard and porch, the Municipal Art Gallery promotes and encourages contemporary artists and celebrates American and Mississippi art.

Municipal Art Gallery of Jackson. *Courtesy of Diane Williams.*

OLD CAPITOL MUSEUM
100 SOUTH STATE STREET
JACKSON, MS 39201

The Mississippi State Capitol is located a few blocks north of its former location. Its former home, the Old Capitol Building, served as the state capitol from 1839 to 1903 before serving as a state office building from 1917 to 1959. Constructed in 1839 in the Greek Revival style, the building is a National Historic Landmark and one of the first museums accredited by the American Association of Museums, in 1972. At the museum's entrance is a rotunda dome towering ninety-four feet. In another room down the corridor, a film provides an excellent overview of the building and its history. Other rooms in this building include lifelike statues that give the appearance of people reciting speeches. Exhibit rooms tell the story of Native Americans' Mississippi history, colonial life, agriculture, regional history, state constitutions and the Civil War. The Hall of Fame recognizes the achievements and contributions of Mississippians.

OLD COURT HOUSE MUSEUM
1008 CHERRY STREET
VICKSBURG, MS 39180

The Old Court House Museum in the old Warren County Courthouse is easy to spot atop the hill overlooking the city. The courthouse, built between 1858 and 1860 by skilled enslaved labor, served the county until 1939. Listed among the twenty most outstanding courthouses in America by the American Institute of Architects, the Warren County Courthouse was known for more than court cases. It hosted famous speakers like Jefferson Davis, Ulysses S. Grant, William McKinley, Teddy Roosevelt and Booker T. Washington. The courthouse, managed by the Vicksburg and Warren County Historical Society, opened as a museum in 1948. Known as the "Crown Jewel of Vicksburg," the museum was listed as a National Historic Landmark in 1968. Within the museum, the McCardle Research Library contains local and county history and family, cemetery, census and marriage records. Also housed here are tax records, Civil War manuscripts, maps, antique furniture, antebellum clothing, pioneer implements, portraits, one of the largest collections of Civil War memorabilia, furniture, china, silver, toys, tools, a cast-iron judge's dais and other historical items and documentation. Exceptional artifacts recount Vicksburg and U.S. history, including rare samples of newspapers printed on sheets of wallpaper during the war, because paper was in short supply. Native American history is reflected in information about the Choctaw Trail of Tears. The gift shop offers artillery shell fragments, lead bullets from the 1863 Battle of Vicksburg, rare historic coins and other items related to Vicksburg's history.

OLD DEPOT MUSEUM
1010 LEVEE STREET
VICKSBURG, MS 39183

Restored by the City of Vicksburg, the Old Depot Museum stands majestically on the banks of the Yazoo River at the mouth of the Mississippi River. Museum souvenirs include clothing, flags, postcards and various memorabilia. Thematically, exhibits relate to water transportation with hundreds of scale-model vessels, boats and ships from the Viking era to the present time. There are more than one hundred models of Civil War gunboats, identified by name. Items related to water transportation and aircraft, as well as giant model railroad and train sections (N, O, HO and O scale layouts) are on view, complete with buildings, scenery and architecture. There are reference materials, maps and a diorama that includes 2,300 miniature soldiers and depicts the forty-seven-day Siege of Vicksburg in a 250-square-foot exhibit of the battlefield. Forty original paintings by Herb Mott depict the trials of the war and are appropriately titled "War on the River." This depiction is known to be the only diorama of the Battle of Vicksburg. A model of fading and long-gone architectural styles reveals designs from shanties to mansions. Other items display the ground war and naval history of the Civil War.

PEMBERTON'S HEADQUARTERS
1018 CRAWFORD STREET
VICKSBURG MS 39183

Born in 1814, John Clifford Pemberton was a West Point Military Academy graduate who served in the Second Seminole War in Florida. He became a brigadier general in the Confederate army, unusual for a northerner, and, as a lieutenant general serving in Mississippi and East Louisiana, oversaw the shipping port of Vicksburg. He defended against the Union attack on Vicksburg but surrendered the city to the United States. Acquired by the National Park Service in 2003, the Pemberton Headquarters building became part of the Vicksburg National Military Park. William Bobb constructed the building in 1835 in the Greek Revival style, popular in Mississippi then. Plans are in place to acquire period furnishings, and once restoration is complete, scheduled for summer 2024, interpretive exhibits will reflect on General Pemberton's victorious hope before he had to surrender the city.

PHILADELPHIA–NESHOBA COUNTY HISTORICAL SOCIETY
303 WATERS AVENUE
PHILADELPHIA, MS 39350

Located in the George Pegram Woodward home since 1992, the museum contains artifacts highlighting the history of the Civil War, notable local musicians and the Neshoba County Fair. Established in 1889, the annual fair, also called "Mississippi's Giant House Party," is an essential part of Mississippi's history and celebrates the state's agriculture and politics. The museum's goal is to "preserve and showcase the heritage and culture of the county." The house contains vintage furniture, memorabilia and photographs. On the site is an original county fair cabin.

RANKIN COUNTY HISTORICAL MUSEUM
1471 WEST GOVERNMENT STREET
BRANDON, MS 39042

Managed by the Rankin County Historical Society, the Rankin County Historical Museum, established in 1981, is behind the Rankin Library in Brandon and includes several other buildings and structures, including the Goshen Springs Post Office, the Atkins-McRae Building, the Neely-Wilson Home, an Old Wagon and Ye Olde Smokehouse.

SAM B. OLDEN YAZOO HISTORIC SOCIETY MUSEUM
332 NORTH MAIN STREET
YAZOO CITY, MS 39194

The Sam B. Olden Yazoo Historic Society Museum is inside the Triangle Cultural Center. The museum building, formerly known as the Main Street School, hosts a variety of activities, such as quilt shows and visual art exhibits, as well as dance, music and art classes. Permanent displays include the William Duke Carter Collection of Antique Tools and contents of the Sam B. Olden Yazoo Historical Society Museum. The museum features a broad array of exhibition topics, including the Civil War era, World War I, the Great Mississippi Flood of 1927, the old Main Street School, political history, local folklife, fossils, Native American relics and African American history. Also highlighted are stories about Willie Morris, comedian and storyteller Jerry Clower, legendary railroad engineer Casey Jones, NFL Hall of Famer Willie Brown, former governor Haley Barbour, Mississippi congressman Mike Espy, Zig Ziglar and many more. Historian, author and world traveler Samuel Olden was also an art collector whose ceramic vessels from ancient Andean cultures are on display at the Mississippi Museum of Art in Jackson, Mississippi.

Sam B. Olden Yazoo Historic Society Museum. *Courtesy of Visit Yazoo.*

Sam B. Olden Yazoo Historic Society Museum. *Courtesy of Visit Yazoo.*

SAMUEL MARSHALL GORE ART GALLERY
MISSISSIPPI COLLEGE
199 MONROE STREET
CLINTON, MS 39058

Mississippi College established the Samuel Marshall Gore Art Gallery between Jefferson and College Streets as a legacy to Samuel Marshall Gore (1927–2019). Gore was the college's first full-time art instructor, his tenure beginning in the early 1950s. He is the recipient of the Mississippi Governor's Award for Career in Art, the Outstanding Citizen of the Year Award from the Clinton Chamber of Commerce, the Ageless Heroes Award for Creativity from Blue Cross/Blue Shield of Mississippi, the Order of the Golden Arrow Award from Mississippi College, a Lifetime Achievement Award and the Mississippi Institute of Arts and Letters Award. To its credit, the gallery has an interesting collection of fine art.

SMITH ROBERTSON MUSEUM AND CULTURAL CENTER
528 BLOOM STREET
JACKSON, MS 39202

In the Historic Farish Street District in Jackson, the Smith Robertson Museum and Cultural Center informs and educates the public on the South, the struggles and achievements of African Americans and the Farish Street Historic District. The museum celebrates Smith Robertson School student Richard Wright, a renowned author and contemporary of Eudora Welty; William Faulkner; and Margaret Walker Alexander. Entering the building, visitors see a sign that reads, "Akwaaba," meaning "welcome" in the Akan (Twi) African language spoken in Ghana. On one side of the foyer, an interpretive exhibit tells the Smith Robertson School story; on the other, the Richard Wright story is told. Visual art and quilts by local artists cover the walls. Two main-floor gallery rooms accommodate changing exhibitions, and presentations and performances take place in the auditorium. The second-floor interpretive African walk-through exhibition conveys the Middle Passage journey of Africans through a slave ship replica and mannequins representing newly enslaved people in the lower deck holding area. The scene creates the emotional darkness of an unknown future. In another room, the Great Migration and the civil rights movement are highlighted. Other displays feature an old-fashioned Black doctor's office and a drinking

Smith Robertson Museum and Cultural Center. *Courtesy of James Patterson.*

fountain depicting an era when whites and Blacks drank from separate fountains in the segregated South. The latter exhibit exposes how a civil rights activist was heckled and traumatized at a lunch counter in the pre–civil rights era while also being refused service as a paying customer. The Medgar Evers Interpretive area in the museum tells the life story of Medgar Evers, a military man, husband, activist and leader. There is a reception hall for events and a gift shop.

TWO MISSISSIPPI MUSEUMS
MUSEUM OF MISSISSIPPI HISTORY
MISSISSIPPI CIVIL RIGHTS MUSEUM
222 NORTH STREET
JACKSON, MS 39201

The Two Mississippi Museums preserve the painful stories and truths of our ancestors and are a testament to our deep resolve to heal our communities. Opening in 2017, the Museum of Mississippi History and the Mississippi Civil Rights Museum are identified as the Two Mississippi

Two Mississippi Museums. Ceremony for the new Mississippi state flag at the Two Museums. *Courtesy of Sarah Warnock.*

*Left*: Two Mississippi Museums. Ceremony for the new Mississippi state flag at the Two Museums. *Courtesy of Sarah Warnock*.

*Below*: Two Mississippi Museums, Mississippi Civil Rights Museum. *Credit: unknown*.

Museums. They share a lobby, auditorium and other areas. In partnership with the Mississippi Department of Archives and History, the Museum of Mississippi History brings to life thousands of years of history through galleries identified by the following titles: The First Peoples (13,000 BC–AD 1518), Cultural Crossroads (1519–1798), Joining the United States (1799–1832), Cotton Kingdom (1833–1865), The World Remade (1866–1902), Promise and Peril (1903–1927), Bridging Hardship (1928–1945),

Forging Ahead (1946-Present) and Reflections. The Mississippi Civil Rights Museum houses eight galleries: Mississippi Freedom Struggle: What It Was All About; Mississippi in Black and White: 1865–1941; This Little Light of Mine: Activists Honored; A Closed Society: 1941–1960; A Tremor in the Iceberg: 1960–1961; I Question America: 1963–1964; Black Empowerment: 1965–mid-1970s; Where Do We Go From Here?: Reflect and Dialogue.

USS *Cairo* Gunboat and Museum
3201 Clay Street
Vicksburg, MS 39180

Just northeast of the National Cemetery at Vicksburg National Military Park, visitors can walk alongside an 1864 gunboat, the USS *Cairo*, named after Cairo, Illinois, along the upper Mississippi and Ohio Rivers. The ship held about 250 men and officers. It was commissioned in January 1862 to spend its time in Tennessee during the Battle of Fort Pillow, scouting the Mississippi River for threats to Confederate supply lines. Struck by two torpedoes in December 1862, the gunboat sank thirty-six feet to a watery grave, left to be forgotten until it was lifted from the Yazoo River in 1966. The ship was taken apart and reassembled. The government authorized the National Park Service to oversee the reconstruction of the vessel. Many artifacts were salvaged from the gunboat and are now on exhibit in the museum next to the ship. They include weapons, munitions, muskets, pistols, medical supplies, food utensils, tools, equipment, an original gun carriage, a ship's bell and items owned by the military. There is a curated history of ironclads and their use in Mississippi and a gift shop where visitors can purchase souvenirs.

Utica Institute Museum
Hinds Community College Campus
34175 MS-18
Utica, MS 39175

The Utica Institute Museum opened in early 2022 on the campus of Hinds Community College–Utica (formerly Utica Junior College). Its purpose is to tell the story of William Holtzclaw, founder of the Utica Institute, and

*This page and opposite*: Utica Institute Museum. *Courtesy of Diane Williams.*

the importance he placed on educating African Americans, as well as the story of the Utica Institute, which was founded in 1903. The museum resides in a small house that consists of a bi-level lecture room, two exhibit galleries and an outdoor area fondly referred to as "the back porch," where intimate lectures and discussions take place. The institute is also involved in genealogy work. There are documents and memorabilia on display. This is where one can learn about the Utica community, Hinds Agricultural High School, Utica Junior College and the Utica Jubilee Singers. Hinds Community College / Utica Campus is highlighted, including information on the "Torchbearers," who were former students and employees of the school. The institute proudly displays images of the Torchbearers: Dr. Rod Paige, former U.S. secretary of education; Dr. Walter Washington, former president of Alcorn State University; Dr. Laurence Clifton Jones, founder and first president of Piney Woods Country Life School; Dr. Beverly Wade Hogan, former president of Tougaloo College; the Honorable Bennie Thompson, Mississippi congressman; and others. The museum hosts traveling and temporary exhibits, such as *A Place for All People* from the Smithsonian's National Museum.

VICKSBURG BATTLEFIELD MUSEUM
4139 I-20 FRONTAGE ROAD
VICKSBURG, MS 39183

The Vicksburg Battlefield Museum is a Union gunboat near the Vicksburg National Military Park. Its goal is to share the Civil War history during the campaign and Siege of Vicksburg in 1863, which lasted forty-seven days. Many citizens hid in the ridges carved out as caves, surviving on peas and rats. The museum stores Civil War gunboat models, two hundred ship models, a miniature layout of the battlefield with 2,300 miniature soldiers and an eight-by-twenty-foot diorama of the siege. Diaries and letters provide insight into this era and time of bravado. A short documentary film completes the storytelling. The museum gift shop offers visitors Civil War souvenirs such as books, posters and replica weapons.

VICKSBURG CIVIL WAR MUSEUM
1123 WASHINGTON STREET
VICKSBURG, MS 39183

The Vicksburg Civil War Museum in the former Corner Drug Store in downtown Vicksburg opened in May 2021 and is owned by Charles Pendleton. The museum displays Pendleton's Civil War collection, which reveals more than one side of the war. Along the walls are quotes, including one from the Declarations of Secession from the Confederate States. Exhibitions present how African Americans were part of history through various perspectives, with details shedding light on enslaved people and their plight and those who fought for the stability of the South. As Pendleton's collection grew, he started a nonprofit to bring awareness of the war's impact on people and the contributions of African Americans. Compilations of items reveal aspects related to the war and to nonmilitary life. These items include weapons, ammunition, gun and artillery shells, uniforms, documents and films. There are also camp supplies, such as coffee pots, musical instruments, period games, cookware and medical equipment. Glass cases hold Sharp, Springfield and other manufacturers' rifles. The venue also includes artillery shells, cannonballs and a replica of a slave cabin with modest furniture. Letters of secession from each Confederate state attest that slavery was the main reason for the war, and a copy of "A Declaration of the Immediate Causes which Induce and Justify the Secession of the State of Mississippi from the Federal Union" lists the refusal of new slave states into the Union and the nullification of the Fugitive Slave Act as reasons for Mississippi's secession. It also rejects "negro equality, socially and politically." The museum displays a bill of sale for Ella, a seven-year-old girl sold in 1848 for $350; an enlistment for the Fifty-Second United States Colored Infantry, with names signed only as "X"; and references to the twenty-five Black men presented the Medal of Honor during the Civil War.

## VICKSBURG NATIONAL MILITARY PARK, VISITORS CENTER / MUSEUM
## 3201 CLAY STREET
## VICKSBURG, MS 39183

The National Park Service manages the Vicksburg National Military Park. Its mission is "to preserve the natural and cultural resources and values of the National Park System for the enjoyment and inspiration of this and future generations," focusing on telling the story of the battles in the city. The Vicksburg Campaign started on May 18, 1863, and ended on July 4. General Ulysses S. Grant and the Union army knew that Vicksburg was a port city on the Mississippi River guarded by the Confederacy. The forty-seven-day battle led to defeat. In the Vicksburg National Military Park Visitors Center, a small museum with several dioramas conveys the Siege of Vicksburg. One reveals how citizens survived in dugout caves; another shows soldiers in the trenches; and another diorama references a field hospital. Civil War artifacts include a military and sword display, an animated light map presentation of the battle, a view of an exterior of a Civil War–era earthen fort and a written and dated account of the battle. Visitors can watch a film about the battle. An artillery display, the antebellum Shirley House, cannons, carriages, the Vicksburg National Cemetery, other historic buildings, four historic fortifications and a reconstructed fort model are on the grounds. The National Park Service provides guided tours.

## WAR MEMORIAL BUILDING
## 120 NORTH STATE STREET
## JACKSON, MS 39201

The War Memorial Building, with its columns standing majestically as if guarding the structure, honors the soldiers lost in battle and gives a brief history of our country. It sits next to the Old Capitol Museum. The unique cast-aluminum doors and panel images tell stories from the Battle of Ackia (1736). On exhibit inside the building are uniforms, weapons, maps, photographs, Medals of Honor and other artifacts from the battlefields of the Spanish-American War, World Wars I and II and the Korean and Vietnam conflicts.

# Part IV

# SOUTHEAST/SOUTHWEST MISSISSIPPI

AFRICAN AMERICAN MILITARY MUSEUM
305 EAST SIXTH STREET
HATTIESBURG, MS 39401

Opened in 1942, during the era of the segregated army of World War II, the USO Club served as a home away from home for African American soldiers stationed at Camp Shelby. This building is the only remaining USO constructed especially for African American soldiers in public use in the United States. It is now listed in the National Register of Historic Places and is a Mississippi Landmark.

Beginning with the Buffalo Soldiers of the post–Civil War era through the modern-day conflicts of Desert Storm and Operation Iraqi Freedom, the museum bears witness to the service and sacrifice of African American soldiers.

African American Military Museum. *Courtesy of Richelle Putnam.*

AFRICAN AMERICAN MUSEUM
222 ROYAL OAKS STREET
WOODVILLE, MS

With extraordinary Federal millwork and mantels and original wood graining, the African American Museum building was initially a Branch Banking House of the State of Mississippi, the Bank of Mississippi, erected in 1819. The Woodmen of the World acquired it in 1912 after an intentional fire destroyed the main building's rear wing, roof and attic. That fire was set in order to destroy evidence of bank fraud and embezzlement. After reconstruction and stabilization by the Civil Club, which acquired the structure in 1973, funds donated by the Woodmen of the World and a Mississippi Department of Archives and History grant, the restoration was completed in 2004.

BAY ST. LOUIS HISTORIC L&N TRAIN DEPOT
ALICE MOSELEY FOLK ART MUSEUM
BAY ST. LOUIS MARDI GRAS MUSEUM
128 DEPOT WAY
BAY ST. LOUIS, MS 39520

The museum is in Bay St. Louis, a quaint town located on the Mississippi Gulf Coast between New Orleans and Mobile. The historic train depot is a 1928 Mission-style, two-story building that once served as the centerpiece of the film *This Property Is Condemned*, starring Robert Redford and Natalie Wood. Now a Mississippi Landmark, the depot houses the Hancock County Tourism office, Bay St. Louis Mardi Gras Museum and Alice Moseley Folk Art Museum. The Bay St. Louis Mardi Gras Museum features an

Alice Moseley's "Blue House." *Courtesy of Richelle Putnam.*

array of elaborate Mardi Gras costumes. The Alice Moseley Museum retains the heritage of folk art and storytelling and celebrates the artist Alice Moseley. In addition to the fifty-two works by Moseley, the museum houses large collections of vintage bottles, Majolica vases, Depression-era

Bay St. Louis Historic L&N Train Depot (Alice Moseley Folk Art Museum and Bay St. Louis Mardi Gras Museum). *Courtesy of Richelle Putnam.*

glass and antique everyday objects. Originally, this museum was in Alice Moseley's "Blue House" on Bookter Street but was relocated to the depot in February 2013.

BLACK HISTORY GALLERY
819 WALL STREET
MCCOMB, MS

Opened in 2001, the Black History Gallery stores and preserves newspaper articles, photos, school yearbooks, magazines and more and contains the most extensive, comprehensive collection of Black history in the region, complete with personal narratives. Here, visitors explore and learn about the Black history of McComb and Pike County, Mississippi. The local author section of books and artwork provides native perspectives about the community, and its many charts capture the connections of the African Diaspora. McComb and surrounding area natives include Bo Diddly and Vasti Jackson, who have carried "Mississippi Blues" worldwide. The Black History Gallery proudly displays these sons and other Black innovators of the past and present.

CAMP VAN DORN WORLD WAR II MUSEUM
138 EAST MAIN STREET
CENTREVILLE, MS 39631

The Camp Van Dorn World War II Museum in Centreville preserves the valuable military history of when the camp was a rigorous training facility for soldiers and the backbone of Centreville. Exhibits contain photos, memorabilia from Camp Van Dorn and items related to war experiences. A collection of over one hundred weekly columns published in local newspapers shares information about the museum, Camp Van Dorn veterans, the camp itself and the war years. The museum provides six printed guides on World War II for educational and instructional purposes: *Wartime Currency in Hawaii and North Africa*; *The Military's Penicillin*; *Rationing in World War II*; *United States History Depicted in the Good Conduct Medal*; *War Bonds*; and *Victory Mail*. Guides are free to teachers and homeschoolers.

CARVER CULTURE MUSEUM
1308 SOUTH HAUGH AVENUE
PICAYUNE, MS 39466

The Carver Culture Museum, a local African American museum in Picayune, Mississippi, contains three major sections: Carver, Picayune and National Black History. The museum preserves the history of George Washington Carver High School (1943–70). The school closed in 1970, when local schools were integrated. The museum also documents the history of Black-owned businesses in Picayune and the many contributions Picayune's Black community has made to Pearl River County.

CROSBY ARBORETUM
370 RIDGE ROAD
PICAYUNE, MS 39466

In the late 1970s, the children of L.O. Crosby Jr. established the Crosby Foundation and Arboretum to honor their father's deep passion for Mississippi nature. Located in Picayune, Mississippi, the facility expanded during the early 1980s, and in 1986, the arboretum was opened to the public. In 1997, the Crosby Foundation partnered with Mississippi

State University, which contributed significant resources to develop the arboretum, a living memorial to the late L.O. Crosby Jr. (1907–1978). Crosby was a prominent forestry figure, civic leader and philanthropist who held a deep compassion for nature. Today, the facility remains owned and operated by MSU as part of its Coastal Research and Extension Center. The facility's mission is to preserve and protect native plants of the Pearl River Drainage Basin Ecosystem and to inform the public about the environment through its many educational and recreational opportunities. A series of exhibits display plant communities typical of southern Mississippi ecosystems. Plans are underway to build a $2 million Education Center.

DE GRUMMOND CHILDREN'S LITERATURE COLLECTION
UNIVERSITY OF SOUTHERN MISSISSIPPI
118 COLLEGE DRIVE, #5148
HATTIESBURG, MS 39406

The de Grummond Children's Literature Collection is one of North America's leading research centers in the field of children's literature. Although the collection has many strengths, the focus is on historical and contemporary American and British children's literature. When Dr. Lena Y. de Grummond came to the University of Southern Mississippi to teach children's literature in the School of Library Science in 1966, she envisioned resources that went beyond the classroom textbook. If students could study the creative processes of authors and illustrators by examining the manuscripts and illustrations firsthand, she knew they would better appreciate the literature. To accomplish this goal, de Grummond wrote to her favorite creators of children's books and solicited contributions of original manuscripts and typescripts, illustrations, sketchbooks, galleys, dummies, publisher correspondence and fan mail—any materials related to the publication of a children's book. Founded in 1966 by de Grummond, the collection holds the original manuscripts and illustrations of more than 1,300 authors and illustrators, as well as more than 180,000 published books from 1530 to the present.

G.I. Museum
5796 Ritcher Road
Ocean Springs, MS 39553

The mission of the G.I. Museum is to preserve memorabilia representing the generations of Americans who served our country. Through displays and educational programs, its goal is to never forget their sacrifice. The museum hosts "Living History" events, in which visitors can come in full-dress uniforms to represent soldiers from the past. The museum also sanctions reenactments and facilitates educational stations for children. In partnership with WKFK Channel 7 in Pascagoula, museum owner Doug Mansfield interviews veterans. This program has earned several Mississippi Association of Broadcasters awards.

Grand Gulf Military Monument Park
12006 Grand Gulf Road
Port Gibson, MS 39150

In May 1962, the Grand Gulf Military Monument Park opened, dedicated to preserving the memory of both the town and the battle that occurred there. This 450-acre landmark is listed in the National Register of Historic Places and includes Fort Cobun and Fort Wade, the Grand Gulf Cemetery, a museum, campgrounds, picnic areas, hiking trails, an observation tower and several restored buildings dating back to Grand Gulf's heyday. Museum items include a mastodon bone, Civil War artifacts and memorabilia from the early 1800s to the 1950s.

Grand Village of the Natchez Indians
400 Jefferson Davis Boulevard
Natchez, MS 39120

The Natchez Indians inhabited Southwest Mississippi from 700 to 1730, when the French forced them from their homeland. The Great Sun's Mound and the Temple Mound were excavated and rebuilt to their original sizes and shapes. The Grand Village of the Natchez on the banks of St. Catherine Creek was the main ceremonial center of the Natchez Nation between 1682 and 1730. This museum and 128-acre park featuring three prehistoric Native American mounds and a nature trail offer a visitor center, a gift shop filled with Native American crafts, a nature trail and an annual Natchez Powwow featuring traditional Native American singing and dancing, foods, crafts and more.

Greene County Museum & Historical Society
400 Main Street
Leakesville, MS 39451

The Greene County Museum & Historical Society maintains and presents the history of Greene County by collecting and preserving historical artifacts, storing and displaying court records and maintaining a genealogical research room.

Hattiesburg Historical Society Museum
Hattiesburg Cultural Center
723 Main Street
Hattiesburg, MS 39401

The Hattiesburg Historical Society Museum collection contains donations from members and friends, including books, magazines, city directories, high school annuals, composite pictures, uniforms, old photographs, furnishings and household goods. The museum also has information related to local industry, small businesses, historic buildings, homes, organizations and individuals. Part of the society's mission is to promote a better understanding

Hattiesburg Historical Society Museum. *Courtesy of Richelle Putnam.*

of American heritage and the democratic way of life. It also seeks to discover, collect and preserve material that helps establish or illustrate the history of Hattiesburg, Forrest County and the surrounding area. This information is available to the public.

HAZLEHURST DEPOT MUSEUM
138 NORTH RAGSDALE AVENUE
HAZLEHURST, MS 39083

The Hazlehurst Depot Museum's mission is to honor and celebrate famous resident Robert Johnson. The museum and the Hazlehurst Chamber of Commerce occupy the historic 1925 train depot, where a 1966 Illinois Central caboose sits nearby on the track. Johnson was born in Hazlehurst, Mississippi, in 1911. As a young musician, he drifted from plantation to plantation in the Mississippi Delta, listening to blues musicians. Legend tells us that Johnson sold his soul to the devil at the crossroads of Highways 61 and 49 so he could play the Delta blues. History tells us that Johnson returned to his Hazlehurst home determined to improve his novice guitar playing with mentors like Ike Zimmerman, who practiced with Johnson in the local cemetery.

HILDA HOFFMAN MEMORIAL ARCHIVE INC.
301 WILLIAMS AVENUE
PICAYUNE, MS 39466

Hilda Formby was born on May 9, 1918. She attended East Side Elementary School and Picayune High School and, after graduation, worked in local businesses until she joined the U.S. Navy in 1940. There she met and married Emile James Hoffmann. The navy enrolled Hilda in special training to learn codes and signals before placing her undercover as a courier of secret documents. (According to Hilda's nephew Lieutenant Colonel Lourie N. Formby III, this story is fictitious.) Her official title was "File Clerk." Her husband was placed in undercover operations by the U.S. Navy. Hilda told of several interesting and sometimes embarrassing situations that occurred during her time in the service. Once, she had to board a ship by climbing a steep ladder wearing a skirt. In another incident, she had to play the role of a prostitute. On delivering secret documents to Canada, Hilda met Prime

Minister Winston Churchill and his son. After the war, Hilda continued her research into the families of Pearl River County residents and amassed a huge archive. Her collection was moved from the metal storage building to a temporary climate-controlled facility in Hancock County until a secure place in Pearl River County could be located. In 2011, Helen Clunie donated a building at 301 Williams Avenue in Picayune to house the collection. At last, Hilda Hoffmann's archive had a home, and the organization had a headquarters to serve the public.

Institute for Marine Mammal Studies
10801 Dolphin Lane
Gulfport, MS 39503

The Institute for Marine Mammal Studies (IMMS) was established in 1984 for the purposes of public education, conservation and research on marine mammals in the wild and under human care. The facility houses an educational museum, a five-hundred-seat arena, classrooms, a state-of-the-art veterinary hospital and the necessary facilities to provide care and rehabilitation for dolphins, sea turtles and other sick and injured marine mammals. Since its inception, IMMS has participated in the National Stranding Network and is the foremost stranding organization in the Mississippi-Louisiana-Alabama region of the Gulf Coast, providing research and advancement opportunities to higher learning institutions.

Landrum's Country Homestead & Village
1356 Highway 15 South
Laurel, MS 39443

Thomas Landrum of Laurel, Mississippi, did not set out to build a village. It just happened.

The village started as a business of handcrafted pine furniture. Today, seventy buildings are on the beautifully landscaped Landrum's Country Homestead & Village. With exhibits, wagon rides, gem mining, nature trails, a Confederate soldier encampment, an Old West Shooting Gallery and a Native American Village, every visitor has the chance to step back into the late 1800s. Through their partnership with the USDA Forest Service and the Mississippi Forestry Commission, the Landrums created

Landrum's Country Homestead & Village. *Courtesy of Richelle Putnam.*

an educational display on the Civilian Conservation Corps and South Mississippi's reforestation history to show the importance of preservation and conservation. There is a nature trail and a small lake with a pier where people can feed the catfish.

## LAUREN ROGERS MUSEUM OF ART
## 565 NORTH FIFTH STREET
## LAUREL, MS 39441

The oldest art museum in Mississippi, Laurel's Lauren Rogers Museum of Art (LRMA), was founded in 1923 as a memorial to Lauren Eastman Rogers, who had died suddenly two years earlier. Rogers was the only heir to his family's timber fortune. In the wake of his death, the family created the Eastman Memorial Foundation "to promote the public welfare by founding, endowing and having maintained a public library, museum, art gallery and educational institution, within the state of Mississippi." The LRMA's Georgian Revival building was designed by Rathbone DeBuys of New Orleans and completed in 1923, with major additions in 1924 and 1983. The museum continues to look for ways to enhance the structure, with a Building Funds for the Arts Grant from the Mississippi Arts Commission and state legislature. Ironwork inside was created by noted craftsman Samuel Yellin. The LRMA was originally both a museum and a public library, but most library holdings not related to art were transferred to the Jones County Library in 1978–79, leaving the museum to focus on promoting, teaching about and exhibiting the fine arts. LRMA maintains five collecting areas: American Art, European Painting, Native American Basketry, Japanese Ukiyo-e Woodblock Prints and

British Georgian Silver. The museum's library is today devoted to art reference books and clipping files, local history archives and a small collection of rare Mississippiana. Highlights of the library collection include a rare 1840 edition of Audubon's *The Birds of America*, first editions of several William Faulkner novels and, more recently, the chandelier installations of renowned glass artist Dale Chihuly. Also on display is Chihuly's fabulous Aventurine Green Chandelier with Copper Leaf and his Laguna Murano Chandelier, installed during the Lauren Rogers Museum's one hundredth anniversary celebration in 2023. The latter piece is considered to be the most important of its type.

Lauren Rogers Museum of Art. *Courtesy of Richelle Putnam.*

Lauren Rogers Museum of Art. *Courtesy of Richelle Putnam.*

LAURENCE C. JONES MUSEUM
5096 HIGHWAY 49 SOUTH
PINEY WOODS, MS 39148

Laurence Clifton Jones established the Piney Woods School in rural Rankin County with two dollars and three students one hundred years ago. Jones began the school in the shade of a cedar tree, with students using a fallen log for a desk. Eventually, Ed Taylor (formerly enslaved) gave Jones forty acres with an abandoned sheep shed, which served as the school's first building. Locals contributed to the growth of the school, which concentrated on vocational skills along with the "three Rs": reading, writing and arithmetic. Over the next twenty years, Jones built the foundation of Piney Woods, beginning with the re-appropriation of the rundown sheep shed. The first building served as a classroom and a dormitory for students from all over Mississippi. In 1929, the school was opened to blind students, offering the only educational opportunity for Mississippi's blind African American community until the state opened a facility in 1950. One of only four historically Black boarding schools in the United States, Piney Woods today continues the tradition of industrial education. In addition to the working farm, the campus has a printing shop, an automotive shop and a daycare facility. Piney Woods provided a model for other educators and leaders throughout the world.

LAWRENCE COUNTY REGIONAL HISTORY MUSEUM
125 EAST BROAD STREET
MONTICELLO, MS 39654

The Regional History Museum depicts the history of Territorial Lawrence County and highlights the St. Stephens Road connecting Fort St. Stephens on the Tombigbee River and intersecting the Pearl River at Monticello. The road served to create the cultural and economic center of Mississippi's early interior county settlements. The museum displays the political and social histories of Lawrence Countians, all remarkable stories of faith and endurance.

Lincoln County Historical & Genealogical Society
227 S. Church Street
Brookhaven, MS 39602

In 1907, Illinois Central constructed the Union Station and freight house in downtown Brookhaven. The town was a hub between the Illinois Central (formerly the New Orleans, Jackson and Great Northern); the Brookhaven and Pearl River Railroad; the Mississippi Central; and the Meridian, Brookhaven, and Natchez Railroad. The F.D. Chase–designed Tudor Revival building is in the National Register of Historic Places and houses the museum, which exhibits artifacts and information about Brookhaven citizens and the military dating back to World War I.

Lucile Parker Gallery
Asbury Academic Building
William Carey University–Hattiesburg Campus
512 Tuscan Avenue
Hattiesburg, MS 39401

The Lucile Parker Gallery celebrates the legacy of Sumrall, Mississippi native Lucile Parker, who earned her bachelor of fine arts degree in drawing and art from the University of Southern Mississippi and her master of arts degree in art, painting and drawing from the University of Alabama. At William Carey, Parker organized the art department and was chairperson from 1974 to 1983. The Lucile Parker Gallery hosts exhibitions of local, state and nationally known artists and houses four permanent collections: the Lucile Parker Collection, the William Carey University Collection, the Larry H. Day Collection and the Brian Blair Collection.

Lynn Meadows Discovery Center
246 Dolan Avenue
Gulfport, MS 39507

The Lynn Meadows Discovery Center opened in 1998 and is dedicated to inspiring children, families and communities through the arts, interactive educational experiences and exploration. Located in the renovated Mississippi City Elementary School, constructed in 1915 and an architectural exhibition itself, the discovery center offers fifteen thousand square feet of indoor exhibit space, seven and a half acres of outdoor play space, a spacious theater, a Viking kitchen and other great facilities for community use. In April 2016, Lynn Meadows Discovery Center was awarded the highest honor a museum can receive, the National Medal for Museum and Library Service. This award, presented by the First Lady of the United States, is given as a tribute to an organization's ability to make a difference in the lives of children, families and communities through extraordinary and innovative approaches to public service, exceeding the expected levels of community outreach. Lynn Meadows Discovery Center was one out of only ten recipients throughout the nation.

Marine Education Center GCRL (Gulf Coast Research
  Laboratory)
101 Sweetbay Drive
Ocean Springs, MS 39564

The Marine Education Center works across the University of Southern Mississippi's Coastal Operations to engage members of diverse communities in ocean sciences, promoting careers and fostering community involvement through formal and informal education programs that provide participants with a better understanding of the Gulf of Mexico. The center promotes an understanding of coastal and marine science within the public sector and provides tools that coastal residents can use to become more effective stewards and advocates for the Gulf of Mexico through innovative, field-based educational experiences. Journeys are made through different coastal habitats, including the sensitive transition from forested bayhead to tidal marsh as seen from the pedestrian suspension bridge on campus.

Marion County Museum
200 2nd Street, #3
Columbia, MS 39429

The Marion County Museum preserves two hundred years of area history. It is located in the old Gulf and Ship Island Railroad passenger depot in Columbia. The museum archives display Native American artifacts and sports and political memorabilia.

Maritime & Seafood Industry Museum
2600 Beach Boulevard
Biloxi, MS 39533

Preserving the hundreds of one-of-a-kind artifacts from the historic Biloxi seafood industry remains the primary function of the Maritime & Seafood Industry Museum, established in 1986. To help interpret Biloxi's and the Mississippi Gulf Coast's maritime history and heritage, there are exhibits on shrimping, oystering, recreational fishing, wetlands, managing marine resources, charter boats, marine blacksmithing, wooden boat building, net making, catboats/Biloxi skiff and a shrimp-peeling machine, a priceless

*This page and opposite*: Maritime & Seafood Industry Museum. *Courtesy of Richelle Putnam.*

photograph and artifact collection tells a history from the first Native American inhabitants to the evolution of a world-renowned seafood processing center. The Wade Guice Hurricane Museum within the museum features exhibit space and a theater. Exhibitions of regional and national maritime artists rotate during the year in the art gallery.

MISSISSIPPI ARMED FORCES MUSEUM
BUILDING 850, FORREST AVENUE
CAMP SHELBY, MS 39407

The Mississippi Armed Forces Museum, located at historic Camp Shelby in Hattiesburg, is the state's largest collection of historic military artifacts from the early nineteenth century to the present. The collection celebrates the State of Mississippi and the brave Mississippian service members who have contributed to the nation's armed forces. Camp Shelby was activated on July 18, 1917, as a training camp for National Guard soldiers during World War I. The army selected names for all the new camps, and the "Hattiesburg Camp" was officially designated Camp Shelby on its activation date to honor Isaac Shelby, a hero of the Revolutionary War and the War of 1812, renowned frontiersman and the first governor of Kentucky.

## MITCHELL FARMS
650 LEAF RIVER CHURCH ROAD
COLLINS, MS 39428

Mitchell Farms was started in 1960 by Dennis and Nelda Mitchell and encompasses 1,500 acres in Southeast Mississippi's piney woods. The setting presents the farm's history and the crops grown there and showcases the cabins, the Banquet Barn and other buildings constructed from the property's timber, which is cut and sized in the Mitchell sawmill. The agritourism initiative, started in 2006, provides firsthand opportunities to learn about farming.

## MOUNT LOCUST
NATCHEZ TRACE PARKWAY, MILEPOST 15.5
NATCHEZ, MS 39120

Mount Locust, constructed about 1780, was an inn and working plantation on the Old Natchez Trace during its heyday. John Blommart started the Mount Locust plantation, but in 1784, his business partner, William Ferguson, purchased it and built the historic house that became an inn for travelers. After William's death and Paulina Burch Ferguson's marriage to James Chamberlain, the home was referred to as the Ferguson-Chamberlain Home. Archaeologists believe that twelve to sixteen slave cabins once occupied the property, each housing four to five enslaved people. Forty-three enslaved people were buried in a cemetery on the land they toiled. Today, Mount Locust is the only surviving inn of over fifty on the Natchez Trace from that bustling period and one of Mississippi's oldest structures. In addition to seeing the inn, visitors can walk the grounds to the enslaved-persons cemetery, the Ferguson-Chamberlain cemetery and the brick kiln site, where enslaved people made the bricks for the Ferguson-Chamberlin Home.

## MUSEUM OF JEWISH EXPERIENCE
213 SOUTH COMMERCE STREET
NATCHEZ, MS 39120

Congregation B'nai Israel in Natchez was founded in 1840 as Chevra Kedusha (Holy Society), and the first synagogue was built in 1867–72 in a restrained Classical style. It was destroyed by fire. The current structure, designed by architect H.A. Overbeck of Dallas, Texas, and constructed in 1904–5, reintroduced Classicism to the religious architecture of Mississippi and is similar in design to the 1906 Hebrew Union Temple in Greenville, also designed by Overbeck. The Natchez Jewish community reached its peak population in 1907 before its slow decline in the remaining twentieth century. In 1992, the congregation entered an agreement with the Museum of the Southern Jewish Experience to share the space and then later conveyed the building to the Goldring/Woldenberg Institute of Southern Jewish Life (ISJL), which maintains it as part of the Museum of the Southern Jewish Experience. The building is a Mississippi Landmark and contributing element no. 96 in the Natchez-on-Top-of-the-Hill Historic District listed in the National Register of Historic Places.

NASA JOHN C. STENNIS SPACE CENTER
INFINITY SCIENCE CENTER
ONE DISCOVERY CIRCLE
PEARLINGTON, MS 39572

The John C. Stennis Space Center dates to 1699, when Indians, settlers, pirates and soldiers shaped the Picayune area of Mississippi. In 1961, the federal government selected Mississippi to be the test facility for launch vehicles to be used in the Apollo missions. Today, it houses many federal and independent contractor projects in the space industry. Opened in 2012, the INFINITY Center is the Stennis Space Center's museum and public education center. Inside, explorers of every age learn about the space program and experience what astronauts did through interactive simulator programs. Although visitors cannot tour the Stennis Space Center, there is a YouTube virtual tour online.

In 2001, a group of visionaries came together and formed a nonprofit foundation with the goal of raising funds to create a science center that would take over much of the StenniSphere mission and serve as a regional focal point for science research and science education. NASA was an early partner in the effort, dedicating 199 leasable acres four miles south of the Stennis Space Center's main entrance, next to the Welcome Center. The seventy-thousand-square-foot INFINITY Science Center now features an education wing, indoor and outdoor artifacts, Earth and space exhibit galleries, theaters, live programs and demonstrations. Educational exhibits draw content from real-life space and ocean exploration activities conducted by the more than thirty labs and offices at the nearby research complex.

## NATCHEZ MUSEUM OF AFRICAN AMERICAN HISTORY AND CULTURE
## 301 MAIN STREET
## NATCHEZ, MS 39120

Created in 1990, the Natchez Association for the Preservation of Afro-American Culture preserves the cultural and historical contributions of Afro-Americans in the growth of Natchez and the nation. The Natchez Museum of African American History and Culture contains exhibits from historic sites, citizens and events connected to Natchez's African American culture. Museum exhibits include the Rhythm Nightclub fire, in which over two hundred African American citizens were burned or trampled to death; and Forks of the Road, the second-largest slave market in the South. Also exhibited are selected literary works of Natchez native and esteemed author Richard Nathaniel Wright. One historic site is the house of freed slave William Johnson (the "Barber of Natchez") on State Street in downtown Natchez, donated to the National Park Service in 1990. In 2005, the park service opened the William Johnson House as a museum and used his diaries from 1830 to 1851 (fourteen leather-bound volumes) to detail his life. The diaries are a critical resource for the study of free Black people, African American history and American history.

## OHR-O'KEEFE MUSEUM OF ART
## 386 BEACH BOULEVARD
## BILOXI, MS 39530

The work of early modernist movement leader and self-proclaimed "Mad Potter of Biloxi" George Ohr rebuffed nineteenth-century American aesthetic norms. Ohr opened his Biloxi Art and Novelty Pottery studio in 1890, but an October 12, 1894 fire burned it and much of Biloxi. Ohr's early blacksmith training influenced the shapes and lines in his curling ribbon handles for vases, teapots and mugs. His brilliantly colored glazes drew widespread attention. His work represented Mississippi at the World's Columbian Exposition in Chicago (1893), the St. Louis World's Fair (1904) and

*This page and opposite*: Ohr-O'Keefe Museum of Art. *Courtesy of Richelle Putnam.*

other world's fairs and expositions. The mission of the Ohr-O'Keefe Museum is to honor, preserve and exhibit Ohr's cultural legacy and critical influence on twentieth- and twenty-first-century art. The Ohr-O'Keefe Museum, designed by one of the twenty-first-century's most admired architects, Frank Gehry, opened in 2010 and is the primary depository in Mississippi for his work.

PEARL RIVER COMMUNITY COLLEGE MUSEUM
HANCOCK HALL
OLD STADIUM DRIVE
POPLARVILLE, MS 39470

Founded as Pearl River County Agricultural High School in 1909, a member of the nation's first state-funded agricultural high school system, Pearl River College is the oldest publicly funded two-year institution of higher learning in Mississippi and the sixteenth oldest in the United States. The Pearl River Community College Museum is a repository for artifacts that reflect the history and legacy of the school and the six-county area that provides financial support for its operation (Forrest, Hancock, Jefferson Davis, Lamar, Marion and Pearl River Counties). The museum is dedicated to the discovery, preservation and interpretation of materials and memorabilia related to the institution's history and the lower Pearl River valley, which it serves. The museum seeks to provide the institution's students, employees, alumni and the public with information regarding the unique history of Pearl River Community College and the history of the supporting district.

ROBERT JOHNSON MUSEUM
218 EAST MARION AVENUE
CRYSTAL SPRINGS, MS 39059

The Robert Johnson Museum, open by appointment only, highlights the life and music career of Robert Johnson, who achieved worldwide renown decades after his death and became known as the "King of the Delta Blues Singers." Johnson's influence touched rock legends like the Rolling Stones, Bob Dylan, Eric Clapton, the Allman Brothers and more. Johnson (1911–1938) recorded twenty-nine songs between 1936 and 1937 for the American Record Corporation, which released eleven 78 rpm records on its Vocalion label during Johnson's lifetime and one after his death. Myths surrounding his life and death include Johnson selling his soul to the devil and being poisoned by a lady friend's jealous boyfriend.

SARAH GILLESPIE MUSEUM OF ART
498 TUSCAN AVENUE
HATTIESBURG, MS 39401

The Sarah Gillespie Collection is a comprehensive and extensive assembly of art executed by Mississippians during the twentieth century. Numbering over six hundred works and including work by artists from every section of the state employing various media and exploring wide-ranging subject matter, the collection is an artistic, social and historical treasure that represents the work, determination and enthusiasm of Sarah Gillespie, who in 1982 began donating works to William Carey College (William Carey University since 2008). She continued throughout her lifetime and bequeathed a large amount to the university. Though the Sarah Gillespie Gallery, located on the Coast Campus of WCU, was destroyed by Hurricane Katrina, the collection has undergone extensive conservation and preservation measures. These measures saved the collection and allowed full representation of Gillespie's intent and life's work.

Sarah Gillespie Museum of Art. *Courtesy of Richelle Putnam.*

Teddy Bear Museum
1299 South Haugh Avenue
Picayune, MS 39466

The Teddy Bear Museum exhibits the world's largest collection of teddy bear items (more than 26,000), including stuffed teddy bears, puppets, animation, books, dishes, movies, bottles, wind-up toys and a history of President Teddy Roosevelt's refusal to shoot a cornered, injured bear during a hunting expedition in Sharkey County, Mississippi. Within the seven fun-filled rooms are a bear-themed bathroom, a bear man cave, two party rooms and a gift shop.

TrainTastic™ Museum
Formerly the Mississippi Coast Model Railroad
615 Pass Road
Gulfport, MS 39507

Richard P. Mueller Jr. and Glenn Mueller Sr. are the visionaries behind TrainTastic™, the largest and most exciting model train museum in the United States. Visitors enjoy seeing the fifty thousand square feet of fun

*This page and opposite*: TrainTastic™ Museum. *Courtesy of Philip Levin.*

along a scenic and interactive route with mini trains traveling throughout the museum to a wonderland along mountain vistas, rivers, coastlines, fields of gold and farms. The museum hosts STEM programs, summer camps, early childhood education programs, hands-on activities and field trips. It also has an outdoor train that children can ride.

USM MUSEUM OF ART
UNIVERSITY OF SOUTHERN MISSISSIPPI
118 COLLEGE DRIVE
HATTIESBURG, MS 39406

The Gallery of Art & Design exhibits works on loan from artists, museums and galleries and showcases both student and faculty exhibitions. The museum manages two traveling shows: the nationally recognized civil rights exhibition *Faces of Freedom Summer: The Photographs of Herbert Randall* and *Drawing on Katrina: Mississippi Children Respond to the Storm*, a collection of forty framed drawings, paintings and collages by South Mississippi children.

The museum and the Art & Design program have hosted lectures and gallery talks by leading figures in the art world, including the Reverend Victoria Jackson Gray-Adams, a pivotal figure in the civil rights movement; William Bailey, the internationally known painter and professor emeritus of Yale University; Thomas Hoving, director emeritus of the Metropolitan Museum of Art, New York; Daniel Piersol, former curator of prints and drawings at the New Orleans Museum of Art and former curator for the Mississippi Museum of Art; Margaret Livingstone, Harvard professor and author of *Vision and Art: The Biology of Seeing*; Faith Ringgold, national story-quilt artist, children's book author and professor at the University of California, San Diego; and most recently the internationally recognized artist and sculptor Christo.

VETERANS MEMORIAL MUSEUM
920 HILLCREST DRIVE
LAUREL, MS 39440

The Veterans Memorial Museum is a six-thousand-square-foot masterpiece nestled among the pines of Jones County. Founded in 1996, the museum houses thousands of military artifacts and memorabilia reflecting the service and sacrifice of countless courageous servicemen and servicewomen. Local veterans, their families and others throughout our nation and abroad donated each treasure on display. The museum is home to an extensive reference library that includes books, periodicals, newspapers, documentaries and movies in the military genre. The museum offers guest speakers, book signings and reenactments and hosts community groups, special events and annual Memorial Day and Veterans Day commemorations.

WALTER ANDERSON MUSEUM OF ART
510 WASHINGTON AVENUE
OCEAN SPRINGS, MS 39564

The nationally accredited Walter Anderson Museum of Art (WAMA), founded in 1991 and located in Ocean Springs, is dedicated to celebrating Walter Anderson and preserving his paintings, drawings, murals, block prints, sculptures, carvings and writings of coastal plants, animals, landscapes and people. WAMA also honors Anderson's brothers, Peter Anderson, master potter and founder of Shearwater Pottery; and James McConnell Anderson, noted painter and ceramist. Since its inception, WAMA has created a vital center for arts enrichment and study through educational activities, publications and exhibitions. WAMA is the only venue accredited by the American Alliance of Museums in the lower six Mississippi counties and one of three statewide. WAMA has served as a working partner in countless efforts to document and preserve the natural environment of the Gulf Coast. Its collection comprises more than one thousand objects owned by the museum and another one thousand on long-term loans from the family.

Walter Anderson Museum of Art. *Courtesy of Richelle Putnam.*

In addition to showcasing the work of the Anderson family, WAMA displays works by visiting artists chosen for an exhibition based on their connection with Walter Anderson's art or philosophies.

Watkins Museum
117 Eureka Street
Taylorsville, MS 349168

The building, constructed in 1901, served as the *Taylorsville Signal* newspaper office until the late 1960s. In 1930, Hattie and Marie Watkins took over the newspaper after the death of their father, James Thomas Watkins, editor of the paper since 1905. Donated to the Town of Taylorsville in 1968, this oldest commercial building in Taylorsville was converted into a museum in 1972. Displays include an 1837 printing press, vintage farm and medical equipment, clothing, typewriters and various magazines and newspapers.

Waveland's Ground Zero Hurricane Museum
335 Coleman Avenue
Waveland, MS 39576

Waveland's Ground Zero Hurricane Museum is a tribute to the strength and beauty of the human spirit. The museum's building, the historic Waveland Elementary School, was the only structure left standing on Coleman Avenue after Hurricane Katrina, making it a testament to survival, as well as a Ground Zero Museum exhibit. Hurricane Katrina, considered the worst

natural disaster in U.S. history, chose Waveland as its ground zero, hurling winds and a tsunami-like surge onto shore and destroying

Waveland's Ground Zero Hurricane Museum. *Courtesy of Richelle Putnam.*

most of Waveland and much of the Mississippi Gulf Coast, including many historic landmarks. Museum exhibits include *Quilt Tales* and *Stories through Fabrics*, a permanent display of Solveig Wells's Katrina Quilt Series. Discovery Alley, which is between the Suga Pop and Waveland Rooms, is an enrichment space for children of all ages, offering interactive learning and experiential activities. The museum's free hurricane simulator allows visitors to test their nerves, and the thirty-seven-foot custom mural teaches kids about hurricane preparation and escape. Kids participate in "I Spy" and "Search and Find" activities, which teach them about the culture of Waveland and the Gulf Coast and natural disasters. Visitors can enjoy activity card challenges and create art pieces.

WEST END FIRE COMPANY NO. 3
1046 HOWARD AVENUE
BILOXI, MS 39530

This fire company began as a volunteer organization in 1883. It became a functioning fire department for the City of Biloxi, known as West End Fire Company No. 3, in 1904. When its usefulness as a fire station was over, the building became a museum dedicated to Biloxi firefighters and their fallen brothers. Its mission is to preserve firefighting equipment and educate visitors via an extensive photograph collection and paraphernalia. The venue is dedicated to educating children on fire prevention and safety.

WILKINSON COUNTY MUSEUM
498 MAIN STREET
WOODVILLE, MS 39669

The museum opened in 1991 in the historic West Feliciana Railroad Company office, built in 1834 on the southeast corner of Courthouse Square. Judge Edward McGehee constructed the West Feliciana Railroad, the third-oldest railroad in America, with the help of Woodville financiers. In 1919, the federal government acquired the property to serve as a United States Post Office. The Woodville Civic Club acquired it in 1971 to save it from demolition and to preserve the building and its history of transporting cotton from Woodville to boats on the Mississippi River at Bayou Sara, Louisiana. The West Feliciana Railroad was also the first railroad to use standard gauge tracks, the first to use cattle guards and the first to issue and print freight tariff bills. The railroad is considered the oldest of its kind in the country.

WILLIAM M. COLMER VISITOR CENTER
GULF ISLANDS NATIONAL SEASHORE, MISSISSIPPI DISTRICT
3500 PARK ROAD
OCEAN SPRINGS, MS 39564

The Mississippi District of the seashore features natural beaches, historic sites, wildlife sanctuaries, islands accessible only by boat, bayous, nature trails, picnic areas and campgrounds. The Davis Bayou Area is the only portion of Gulf Islands National Seashore in Mississippi accessible by automobile. Petit Bois, Horn, East Ship, West Ship and Cat Islands are accessible only by boat. The 4,080-acre Gulf Islands Wilderness offers special protection, within the seashore, to parts of Petit Bois Island and Horn Island, Mississippi. The William M. Colmer Visitor Center houses exhibits and offers a variety of books, posters, educational games and a park-oriented film to educate and enhance visitors' experience.

Part V

# MUSEUM TOUR HOMES AND HOUSES

A.H. Longino House
130 Caswell Street
Monticello, MS 39654

Monticello was the home of Andrew H. Longino, a Lawrence County native who was the thirty-fifth governor of Mississippi. He was the first governor of Mississippi elected after the Civil War who was not a Confederate veteran. At the turn of the twentieth century, Longino's administration passed the bill for the New Capitol, and the cornerstone was laid in 1903, while Longino was still in office. During his administration, the Mississippi Department of Archives and History was created, as well as the penitentiary at Parchment Farm. He invited President Theodore Roosevelt to Mississippi to go bear hunting.

Amos Deason Home
410 Anderson Street
Ellisville, MS 39437

The Deason Home was completed in 1845, making it the oldest standing home in Jones County. The first inhabitants, Amos and Eleanor Deason, owned seven hundred acres in what is now Ellisville. Originally a farmhouse, the house was the first painted home in the area. Newton Knight, the self-proclaimed governor of the "Free State of Jones," is said to have entered the

Amos Deason Home. *Courtesy of Richelle Putnam.*

home and shot Major Amos McLemore during the Civil War. McLemore's blood seeped into the wood floor. The family could not remove the stain, so they installed another layer of flooring on top of the first to cover the stain. Newton Knight was never charged with the crime. A 2016 movie, *Free State of Jones*, noted Newt Knight's opposition to slavery. The Deason Home is one of the most haunted houses in Mississippi.

## ANTEBELLUM DAVIS HOUSE, STRAWBERRY PLAINS AUDUBON CENTER
## 285 PLAINS ROAD
## HOLLY SPRING, MS 38635

The Davis House, built in 1851 by Ebenezer Nelms Davis, is a restored Greek Revival mansion with its front pedimented portico donning a prominent lunette dormer supported by Corinthian columns. It was called Strawberry Plains, because wild strawberries grew throughout the acreage. Union soldiers raided the plantation during the Civil War, and it lay in ruins for over one hundred years. In the 1970s, Dr. John Shackelford and Margaret Finley Shackelford restored the house and donated it to the National Audubon Society in 1998. The Strawberry Plains Audubon

Center was created, and the three thousand acres became a nature and wildlife center. It serves as an environmental education center, a wildlife habitat and a wedding and event venue.

BACK IN THE DAY MUSEUM
204 YOUNG STREET
GREENWOOD, MS 38930

The museum, an old shotgun house in Greenwood where, it is said, Robert Johnson spent some time, opened in 2006. The museum's purpose is to preserve the history and heritage of Baptist Town and to give visitors a glimpse of a local musician's life. The sign in front reads, "Back in the Day." Inside the faded, worn structure, a guitar leans on a chair in one corner, accompanied by a pot-bellied stove, pictures on the wall, a record player and albums and a collection of drinking glasses on a shelf. In the sewing area are a sewing machine, thread and other sewing items.

BEAUVOIR, THE JEFFERSON DAVIS HOME AND PRESIDENTIAL LIBRARY
2244 BEACH BOULEVARD
BILOXI, MS 39531

In 1877, Jefferson Davis came to the Mississippi Gulf Coast to write his memoirs. He visited childhood friend Sarah Dorsey, who showed him the perfect place to write: her east cottage at Beauvoir. Dorsey had bought the property from Madison County planter James Brown, who obtained the property in 1848 to construct a summer home. Dorsey named the home "Beauvoir" because of its beautiful view. Brown hired skilled artisans from Biloxi and New Orleans, and his Madison County plantation staff and enslaved people performed much of the labor. At Brown's nearby sawmill in Handsboro, workers processed cypress and longleaf heart pine for use in construction. Material importations included roof slate from Wales and marble and etched glass from Italy. Brown elevated the house to allow sea breezes to pass under, around and through it as a cooling mechanism and to save the home from storm surges. Brown completed his vacation home and two small cottages and named it "Orange Grove" for the Satsuma orange groves growing there. Jefferson Davis rented the east cottage from Sarah Dorsey for fifty dollars a month for two years. He purchased the entire

Beauvoir property on February 9, 1879, and it became the "Mount Vernon of the Confederacy." Here, Davis wrote his two-volume memoir, *The Rise and Fall of the Confederate Government*. On site are the Jefferson Davis Presidential Library, Beauvoir Museum, Beauvoir Memorial Cemetery, Oyster Bayou, Mrs. Varina's Garden and historical cottages.

ELVIS PRESLEY BIRTHPLACE
306 ELVIS PRESLEY DRIVE
TUPELO, MS 38801

The Elvis Presley Birthplace highlights the life of the musician and dedicates itself to the preservation of information and items from his early childhood. The museum's event center has space for small group meetings, a theater with a stage and projector screen and a gift shop with over two thousand souvenir items. On the park grounds is a statue of the thirteen-year-old Elvis dressed in overalls, which was unveiled in 2002. Other statues are *Becoming*, which depicts Elvis sitting on a crate with his guitar and Elvis as a grown man with his arms outstretched, head reared back and gazing to the sky. There is an amphitheater for outdoor concerts, the Bridge over Troubled Waters, the Fountain of Life, a Reflections Pond and an Overlook. Here, visitors also find Presley's 450-square-foot childhood home, an outhouse, Elvis's childhood church (the Assembly of God Pentecostal Church) and a park.

ETHEL WRIGHT MOHAMED STITCHERY MUSEUM
307 CENTRAL AVENUE
BELZONI, MS 39038

The Ethel Wright Mohamed Stitchery Museum takes visitors into Ethel Wright's home, where they view her "memory pictures," designs that chronicled stages in her life: childhood, marriage, eight children, community events, history, culture and more. These designs resemble fabric paintings that spur feelings of warmth and tranquility. Ethel Wright and her Lebanese husband and businessman, Hassan Mohamed, operated the Mohamed Store in Belzoni. After her husband's passing in 1965, Ethel continued operating the store, working on her tapestries in her spare time. Between the ages of sixty and eighty-five, she created approximately 125 designs, which achieved prominence in 1974 during the Smithsonian Institution's Festival of American Folklife in Washington, D.C. The Smithsonian also commissioned a tapestry from Wright for the Bicentennial Festival of American Folklife. In 1991, she received the Governor's Lifetime Achievement Award for Excellence in the Arts, awarded through the Mississippi Arts Commission.

EUDORA WELTY HOUSE
1119 PINEHURST STREET
JACKSON, MS 39205

The Eudora Welty House, a 1925 Tudor Revival house, is in the National Register of Historic Places. The captivating Pinehurst Street setting includes gardens, the Welcome Center and a gift shop next door to the house. Exhibits highlight Eudora Welty's awards and reflect on her life. Exhibits at the Welcome Center reproduce Welty's journey, from childhood to international acclaim as an award-winning author. She was the first living author to be included in the Library of America Series. Her legacy offers educational opportunities for K–12 students and teachers. Fellowships, internships and scholarships are unique ways of perpetuating her literary vision. The Eudora Welty Collection is available at the Mississippi Department of Archives and History.

GOVERNOR'S MANSION
300 EAST CAPITOL STREET
JACKSON, MS 39201

The Governor's Mansion, a national landmark, has been home to Mississippi's governors since 1842. Designed by architect William Nichols, a native of Bath, England, the mansion is a perfect example of the Greek Revival style in the United States and is the second-oldest continuously occupied residence for state leaders. The State Dining Room, Gold Parlor and Green Room are highlighted by artifacts, artworks and period furniture. In the Gold Bedroom is an 1850 sofa that belonged to Governor Benjamin G. Humphrey (served 1865–68). The City of Jackson became known as Chimneyville, because much of the city was burned during the Vicksburg Campaign in the summer of 1863. The mansion survived. During the holidays, the mansion hosts Christmas tours. A tour of the gardens is another favorite.

## Heflin House Museum
## 304 South Main Street
## Sardis, MS 38666

The Heflin House Museum is mentioned in *Buildings of Mississippi* (2020), under the listing for the Kyle-Spencer House, NC5, and was built in 1858. It is an antebellum home in the Greek Revival style. It was built by Captain W.D. Heflin, Confederate army quartermaster in Ballentine's Battalion (attending the battles in Iuka, Corinth and Coffeeville). The museum is open for tours every third Sunday of the month and is managed by the Heflin House Museum Heritage organization. Inside, you will find furnishings and objects from the 1800s.

## Holloway-Polk Historical House and Cultural Center
## 6162 Highway 84
## Prentiss, MS 39474

Holloway-Polk House is the oldest continuously inhabited settlement in Jefferson Davis County and the community's only remaining antebellum structure. The house is listed in the National Register of Historic Places. In the early 1900s, African Americans purchased land in Mount Carmel and surrounding area and developed a thriving self-contained community with essential services and goods. The mission of the Holloway-Polk House Historical and Cultural Center is to preserve the house and its historical significance and to be a resource through guided tours and presentations to schools and other public entities.

## Ida B. Wells Barnett Museum
## 220 North Randolph Avenue
## Holly Springs, MS 38635

The museum is located inside the Spires Bolling House in the town where Ida B. Wells was born. The museum includes heirlooms and artifacts of historic value. The Ida B. Wells-Barnett Room contains a collection of personal memorabilia, awards and items that belonged to Wells. The Local Genealogy Room contains information on several African American families who hailed from Holly Springs. There is an art gallery celebrating the works of educators, artists and civic leaders. The museum hosts tours, exhibits, community programs, multicultural programs and theater presentations. The site celebrates the accomplishments of not only Wells but also other notable African Americans. The house is the perfect place for this museum. Ida's father, Jim Wells, born into slavery, had something to do with the construction of the Spires Bolling House. Her mother was the property cook and was well known for her appetizing meals. The site serves as a historic cultural center for the community.

JACQUELINE HOUSE AFRICAN AMERICAN MUSEUM
1325 MAIN STREET
VICKSBURG, MS 39180

Founded in 1995 by Tillman and Dorothy Whitley, Josephine Calloway, Leona Barnes Stringer and Yolande Robbins (Jacqueline's sister), the museum on Main Street is operated by the Vicksburg African American Historical Preservation Foundation. It serves as a repository for the public to study and research African Americans who lived in Vicksburg and Warren County during African American enslavement and the Jim Crow South. The information encompasses the culture and community of Black people through photographs, books, manuscripts, music, posters, newspapers and other artifacts.

JOHN FORD HOME
150 JOHN FORD HOME ROAD
SANDY HOOK, MS 39478

The John Ford Home (Ford's Fort), the oldest frontier-style structure in the Pearl River valley, served as a territorial military post, inn and post office. A Methodist minister, Ford was elected to the South Carolina legislature in 1798 and served two terms. His brother Joseph operated Ford's Ferry on the Pearl River, a critical crossing in its era. During the War of 1812 and the Creek War of 1813, John Ford erected a stockade at his home to protect his family and community.

JOHN HOLLIDAY HOUSE (HOLLIDAY HAVEN)
609 SOUTH MERIDIAN STREET
ABERDEEN, MS 39730

The Holliday Haven is a historic mansion built about 1850 for John Holliday (1803–1881), a native of North Carolina who owned a plantation west of Aberdeen. His wife, Maria Grimes Speight Holliday, was the daughter of Senator Jesse Speight, a North Carolina and Mississippi politician. Holliday Haven is one of the great mansions of Monroe County because of its excellent Greek Revival architecture. The double columns run the entire height of the structure. The house (sometimes spelled "Holiday") has maintained its original furnishings and was listed in the National Register of Historic Places in 1988.

KATE LOBRANO HOUSE
HANCOCK COUNTY HISTORICAL SOCIETY
108 AND 109 CUE STREET
BAY ST. LOUIS, MS 39520

The Hancock County Historical Society is headquartered in the Kate Lobrano House, "a delightful 1896 shotgun cottage that was donated to the society in 1988 by the grandchildren of Katherine Maynard Lobrano." The original house (108 Cue Street) is used as a turn-of-the-century museum. The Kate Lobrano House was constructed in the traditional shotgun style. The Victorian architecture is accented with extensive displays of historic photos of the area. There are turn-of-the-century furnishings in the parlor, and displays include Indian artifacts.

LAPOINTE-KREBS HOUSE AND MUSEUM (OLD SPANISH FORT)
4602 FORT STREET
PASCAGOULA MS 39567

The LaPointe-Krebs Museum displays the history of the LaPointe-Krebs House and the diverse people who inhabited the area. This early residential settlement dates to 1715, when Joseph Simon de La Pointe received a land grant from King Louis XIV for a holding on the Pascagoula River. Hugo Ernestus Krebs, La Pointe's son-in-law, inherited the land in 1751 after marrying Maria Josephine Simon La Pointe in 1741. Constructed in the 1750s, the LaPointe-Krebs House is the oldest standing structure in Mississippi and the oldest between the Appalachians and the Rockies. A 1768 map refers to the Krebs Plantation and its two-story house, slave cabins, kitchen, warehouse, milk house, forge, pigeon house and wooden palisades. The LaPointe-Krebs grounds overlook the Pascagoula River and are perfect for outdoor events like parties, weddings, receptions, fundraisers and concerts. The Krebs Cemetery Tour is held on this site annually on the Thursday before Halloween.


LONGWOOD
140 LOWER WOODVILLE ROAD
NATCHEZ, MS 39120


Unlike other antebellum homes restored and furnished with replicas from the antebellum era and opened as bed-and-breakfasts to travelers, Longwood remains a ghostly reminder of the wealth made possible by the backbreaking labor of enslaved people on plantations and the repercussions of the American Civil War in the South. In 1858, Dr. Haller Nutt began Longwood's construction as a gift for his wife, and the Civil War stopped it. However, only the basement of the largest octagonal mansion in America was complete when the Pennsylvania architect and his artisans and workers left to join the Union army. The unfinished mansion, constructed of over one million bricks, became known as "Nutt's Folly." Five original plantation outbuildings still standing are the necessary privy, kitchen, slave quarters, stables and carriage house. The Pilgrimage Garden Club of Natchez operates the National Historic Landmark as a museum and offers tours.


L.Q.C. LAMAR HOUSE
616 NORTH FOURTEENTH STREET
OXFORD, MS 38655


In 1869, Lucius and Virginia Lamar began construction of the L.Q.C. Lamar House, which was completed in 1870. Listed as a National Historic Landmark and restored in 2008, the house site is owned by the City of Oxford. Each room represents a theme: (1) Family: Land, Slaves and Cotton, (2) War, (3) Reunion, (4) Political Courage and (5) Oratory. The museum explores the politics of slavery, secession and reunion. A bronze statue of L.Q.C. Lamar sits in front of the museum. Its mission is "to interpret the life and career of the distinguished 19th-century statesman L.Q.C. Lamar within the context of his times and to encourage the ideal of statesmanship in the 21st century." A great time to visit is during Oxford's Double Decker Festival.

Magnolia Hall
215 South Pearl Street
Natchez, MS 39120

Around 1858, Natchez native Thomas Henderson, a merchant and wealthy cotton broker, began construction on his residence, Magnolia Hall, the last mansion built in downtown Natchez. The plaster magnolia blossoms in the parlor ceiling centerpieces inspired the home's name. The Natchez Garden Club restored the home and operates it as a house museum, complete with pilgrimage costumes, a doll collection and a gift shop.

The Magnolias
732 Commerce Street
Aberdeen, MS 39730

Five generations of the Sykes family lived at the Magnolias prior to it being sold and then donated to the City of Aberdeen. Planter and physician Dr. William Alfred Sykes (1798–1873) built the house in 1850 for himself and his wife. She died shortly after moving there. William eventually remarried and raised his children there. The antebellum structure is a Greek Revival house with a columned front portico. The grounds include beautiful magnolia trees, azaleas and a rose-covered arbor. Inside is a breathtaking mahogany double staircase and a Waterford chandelier that can be seen from the foot of the stairs. The home reflects life in the mid-1800s with period furnishings and a detached kitchen.

MANSHIP HOUSE MUSEUM
420 EAST FORTIFICATION STREET
JACKSON, MS 39202

Charles Henry Manship built the Manship House in 1857, a few short years prior to the Civil War. Born in Maryland in 1812, Manship was a builder, chair maker, painter and shop owner who sold paints and fine wallpaper. He moved to Jackson during the 1830s building boom. Manship also worked on the construction of the first state capitol, now the Old Capitol Museum. The Mississippi Department of Archives and History's goal has been to restore the house to its 1888 facade, and the work continues. It has been restored to its original color (olive and cream), and the roof shingles have been reproduced. The interior includes a parlor, sitting room, dining room, three bedrooms and a bathing room (a special privilege for the period). The furnishings of the house are in storage and can be viewed by appointment only.

MCRAVEN HOUSE
1445 HARRISON STREET
VICKSBURG, MS 39180

The McRaven House is listed in the National Register of Historic Places. *National Geographic* called it the "Time Capsule of the South," and it is often referred to as one of the most haunted houses in Mississippi and the third-most-haunted house in America (https://hauntedhouses.com/mississippi/mcraven-house). Built as a small, modest home in 1797 when Vicksburg, Mississippi, was known as Walnut Hills, the house went on to serve as a temporary field hospital, an infirmary of sorts, for wounded soldiers during the Civil War. The house's three-phase construction and additions include Frontier, Empire and Greek Revival designs.

MEDGAR AND MYRLIE EVERS HOME NATIONAL MONUMENT
2332 MARGARET WALKER ALEXANDER DRIVE
JACKSON, MS 39204

The Medgar and Myrlie Evers House is also known as the Medgar and Myrlie Evers National Monument, as designated by the National Park

Service. Medgar and Myrlie were civil rights activists who worked with the NAACP. The house is preserved and restored to its appearance when the couple and their three children lived there. The home is a modest, three-bedroom, ranch house built in 1956 on what was formerly known as Guynes Street in the Elraine subdivision of Jackson. Writer Margaret Walker Alexander was the first African American to move into the subdivision when it was developed in 1955. Because of the danger of assassination, the front entrance does not face the street; instead, Medgar opted to create a side entrance through the carport. The home is listed in the National Register of Historic Places and is owned by the National Park Service. The sign under the carport explains Medgar Evers's assassination.

MELROSE MANSION
122 MELROSE AVENUE
NATCHEZ, MS 39120

In 1990, the National Park Service acquired the Greek Revival Melrose estate, a suburban residence for the wealthy lawyer and cotton planter John T. McMurran, his family and the 22 enslaved people who lived and worked there. McMurran owned or co-owned five cotton plantations that prospered from the labor of over 350 enslaved people. His architect, Jacob Byers, used master Irish brickmasons and skilled enslaved laborers to build Melrose's main house and outbuildings. The brickwork is said to be the best in Mississippi and perhaps even in the country. Today, the home illuminates the daily lives of the southern planter class and the enslaved persons who powered the lucrative cotton-based economy of Mississippi before the Civil War. A National Historic Landmark, Melrose showcases its architecture, collection of outbuildings and the mansion's original fine and decorative arts.

MERREHOPE
905 MARTIN LUTHER KING JR DRIVE
MERIDIAN, MS 39301

In 1968, the Meridian Restorations Foundation was formed by the members of the nine Federated Women's Clubs of Meridian. The foundation purchased the Merrehope home, and restoration has been ongoing ever since. Merrehope sits on the 700 acres first owned by Meridian settler

Merrehope. *Courtesy of Richelle Putnam.*

Richard McLemore. In 1858, he deeded 160 acres to his daughter Juriah as a wedding gift. She and her husband, W.H. Jackson, built a Greek Revival cottage. This is the antebellum section of Merrehope. Around 1868, cotton broker John Gary bought and remodeled the home in the Italianate style, adding ruby etched glass around the front door, the double parlor, the library and four rooms upstairs. Between 1881 and 1903, a coal dealer, J.C. Lloyd, his wife and thirteen children lived in the home. Sam Floyd, a wealthy cotton broker from Shubuta, owned the home from 1903 to 1915 and installed electricity. He also added the front columns, balcony, five bathrooms, the walnut hand-carved stairway, the dining room, the morning room and two bedrooms upstairs in Neoclassical style. Merrehope hosts club meetings and can be rented for weddings, receptions and parties. It offers daily tours and presents the annual Trees of Christmas.

MISSISSIPPI JOHN HURT MUSEUM
COUNTY ROAD 109
CARROLLTON, MS 38917

The museum is between Greenwood and Grenada in Carroll County in Avalon, a town so small it is not listed on a map. Access to the museum is via a long dirt path on County Road 109. Blues musician John Hurt grew up in

Avalon, and his childhood home, a humble, three-room shack with a lopsided porch and tin roof, is the museum. A tour of the venue includes visiting the home, church, historical markers, gravesite and old Valley (community) Store. John Hurt and his family are buried near the Valley Store in Avalon on the side of a steep hill leading to the St. James Cemetery.

## Oakes African American Cultural Center
### 312 South Monroe Street
### Yazoo City, MS 39194

In 1853, the African American Oakes family moved to Mississippi. John Oakes, a free Black man, purchased the freedom of his wife and two children from slavery and bought a small plot of land in Yazoo City, Mississippi. In 1866, he built a one-room house that the family expanded into a beautiful two-story home, which has become the Oakes African American Cultural Center. The center highlights the Oakes family history, which is a testament to a successful Black man and his family. The museum exhibits include family letters and business papers spanning several generations celebrating the family. The facility celebrates other African American artists and craftspeople as well, with works of art, photographs, wood sculpture, basketry and quilts. African American achievements highlight local doctors, writers, musicians and others. The center hosts permanent, visiting and traveling exhibits, along with lectures, classes and other programming.

## Oaks House Museum
### 823 Jefferson Street
### Jackson, MS 39202

Constructed in 1853 in the Greek Revival style, the Oaks House survived the burning of Jackson during the Civil War and is one of the oldest homes in the capital city. Listed in the National Register of Historic Places, it was also known as the Boyd House, named after the family of former Jackson mayor James Hervey Boyd, who served four two-year terms. Two unique aspects of the Oaks House Museum are the gardens and the reconstructed milk house, which very few homes in the South had before refrigeration. The Oaks House Museum Corporation manages the museum with a mission "to preserve and interpret the circa 1853 Oaks House, its collection, and grounds, to depict the life of a middle-class family in the mid-19th-century." Some furnishings were crafted by the State Penitentiary Manufacturing Division, once located in Jackson.

PLEASANT REED HOUSE
386 BEACH BOULEVARD
BILOXI, MS 39530

Pleasant Reed was born into slavery in 1854 to his enslaved parents, Charlotte and Benjamin Reed, on John B. Reed's plantation in Perry County, Mississippi. After emancipation, some of Pleasant Reed's family members settled in Biloxi, and he joined them in 1869. Reed married Louisiana native Georgia Anna Harris in 1884 and worked as a carpenter and fishnet maker. He built his family home from his earnings. It is one of the first documented houses built and owned outright by a formerly enslaved person in Biloxi. The altered side hall and camelback Creole cottage allowed for cross-ventilation and privacy within the small space. Reed added an attached kitchen and decorative details to the house, luxuries evidencing the family's increasing financial stability. In the early 1900s, the Reeds were one of Biloxi's most

Pleasant Reed House. *Courtesy of Richelle Putnam.*

prosperous African American families. The house remained in the Reed family until the Mississippi Gulf Coast Alumnae Chapter of Delta Sigma Theta Sorority took ownership in 1978. In 2000, the sorority donated the home, one of the remaining few identified with an African American builder and homeowner, to the Ohr-O'Keefe Museum, which restored it to its circa 1910 appearance. In 2005, Hurricane Katrina destroyed the Pleasant Reed House. In 2008, the Ohr-O'Keefe Museum of Art completed the house replica to serve as an interpretive center honoring the Reed legacy and exhibiting the archives recovered from the house after Hurricane Katrina.

ROSALIE MANSION AND GARDENS
100 ORLEANS STREET
NATCHEZ, MS 39120

Rosalie Mansion sits on a Mississippi River bluff in Natchez. As one of the city's most historic homes, Rosalie was built by lumber mill owner and planter Peter Little, who had purchased twenty-two acres, known as the "Old Fort," for $3,000. The French had established the fort on the land in 1716 and named it Rosalie, after the countess of Pontchartrain. Little completed the house in 1823 and kept the name. Its architecture falls into the Early Classical Revival or Federal period. Peter and his wife, Eliza, lived there until their deaths, hers in 1853 and his in December 1856. Mr. and Mrs. Andrew Wilson acquired the house in 1857. Very few items in the place today belonged to Peter and Eliza Little. But there are portraits of Peter and Eliza, Eliza's locking tea caddy on the table, the Little family Bible on the bookstand, a sampler that sixteen-year-old Eliza stitched in 1809 and Peter's checkbook from 1832. Most furnishings and accessories belonged to the Wilsons, such as the Wilson family books, the smoking stand and a hand-painted Japanese tilt-top table purchased in Asia by a family member. The Cornelius and Baker chandelier is the only original fixture from the Wilson years in the house. Other impressive displays include Italian marble and coal-burning fireplaces and French gilded mirrors. There are two pianos, one a Chickering purchased in the 1880s and the other a French Pleyel (patented 1849). The Wilsons' music books date to 1830. A detailed description of the contents of each room can be downloaded from the Rosalie Mansion and Gardens website. Rosalie has been owned, maintained and operated by the Mississippi State Society Daughters of the American Revolution since 1938.

ROSEMONT PLANTATION
HIGHWAY 24 (JUST OFF HIGHWAY 61)
WOODVILLE, MS

Samuel and Jane Davis built Rosemont Plantation in 1810, when they moved to Wilkinson County, Mississippi, with two-year-old Jefferson Davis. The house they initially called Poplar Grove was renamed Rosemont to honor the rose gardens of Jane Cook Davis. Although there is no architect of record, the vernacular Mississippi planter's cottage design possesses an unexpected central gable and detailed Palladian window. Its interior incorporates the Federal and Greek Revival period. Many Davis family furnishings remain in the house, some donated by members of the Davis family. The grounds and outbuildings, restored by Beacroft and Ernesto Caldeira, create an exceptional timepiece atmosphere, like the Davis family cemetery on the property, serenely resting beneath the ancient oaks and poplars.

ROWAN OAK
916 OLD TAYLOR ROAD
OXFORD, MS 38655

The Rowan Oak house sits on four acres of a twenty-nine-acre property in Oxford, Mississippi. Constructed in 1848, the Greek Revival main house was originally known as the Bailey Place. Recipient of the Nobel Prize, Pulitzer Prize and National Book Award, William Cuthbert Faulkner purchased it in 1930. He changed the name to recognize the Celtic legend of the rowan tree, which says the tree harbors magic powers of safety and protection. Faulkner added the servant's quarters and a stable for his horses and planted a scuppernong arbor to harvest the muscadine-like fruit for jellies and wine. He planted an English Knot Garden, an east wall for privacy and a concentric circle garden. The early 1840s post oak barn was used by Faulkner to house cows and tools. Faulkner turned the original detached kitchen into a smokehouse and added an indoor kitchen. He did much of his writing at Rowan Oak until his death in 1962. Today, the University of Mississippi owns Rowan Oak, now a National Literary Landmark.

## Stanton Hall
401 High Street
Natchez, MS 38120

Stanton Hall, a magnificent, palatial Greek home, occupies an entire city block in downtown Natchez. Standing five stories tall, the house was originally fourteen thousand square feet and still possesses many original furnishings, beautiful antiques and one-of-a-kind arched millwork. A National Historic Landmark, Stanton Hall is owned and maintained by the Pilgrimage Garden Club. Irishman Fredrick Stanton built the massive structure of Greek Revival architecture between 1851 and 1857, accessorizing its interior with carved Carrara marble mantels, French chandeliers cast in bronze and Sheffield silver hardware. A Natchez newspaper describing Stanton Hall in 1858: "All the work on the edifice was done by Natchez architects, builders, artists and finishers." Stanton initially named his home Belfast, after his birthplace. Stanton Hall houses period antiques and architectural features from the antebellum period, but also original Stanton family pieces.

## Stephen D. Lee Home & Museum and Florence McLeod Hazard Museum
316 Seventh Street North
Columbus, MS 39701

Major Thomas Garton Blewett and his wife, Regina DeGraffenreid, built the home in 1847. Through marriage and inheritance, it became the home of General Stephen D. Lee, who had married the granddaughter of Major Blewett. Lee's son later sold the home to the City of Columbus, and it is featured in the Columbus Annual Spring Pilgrimage. The Lee Home is listed in the National Register of Historic Places and is a National Historic Landmark. The museum includes artifacts and collectibles from the Civil War, as well as items of local and regional history, with some items dating back to 1833.

TEMPLE HEIGHTS MANSION
515 NORTH NINTH STREET
COLUMBUS, MS 39701

Built in the Federal and Greek Revival styles in 1837, the house sits on a grassy hill. Temple Heights Mansion was built for Richard Thomas Brownrigg (1793–1846). He was a farmer and general in the army. Temple Heights has been featured in publications such as *The Magazine Antiques*, *Historic Architecture in Mississippi*, *Old Homes of Mississippi Volume 2: Columbus and the North*, *Reflections of Home* and *History of Columbus, Mississippi* and on HGTV's *Old Homes Restored*. The mansion was listed in the National Register of Historic Places in 1978. Its colorful history celebrates its many ghosts, each with a name and story. To learn more about spirits haunting the mansion, visit the website https://hauntedhouses.com/mississippi/temple-heights-mansion.

TENNESSEE WILLIAMS RECTORY MUSEUM
106 SHARKEY AVENUE
CLARKSDALE, MS 38614

The museum covers the four upstairs bedrooms of the former St. George's Episcopal Church rectory. The church remains active today. Thomas Lanier Williams III, known as Tennessee Williams, the author and playwright, was born in Columbus, Mississippi, and lived there for three years until he moved to Clarksdale to live with his grandfather Walter Edwin Dakin, the church rector. From 1917 to 1921, Williams lived in Clarksdale with his family in the rectory of St. George's Episcopal Church. Coahoma Community College hosts an annual three-day Mississippi Delta Tennessee Williams Festival during the month of October. The long-standing event is more than thirty years old and features plays, films, contests, monologues, scholar presentations and more.

TURNER HOUSE MUSEUM
500 BAY STREET
HATTIESBURG, MS 39401

Turner House Museum, Hattiesburg's only house museum, promotes research and public education through its exhibits, events and educational programs. The house was built about 1890–1910 as a wedding gift for Annie Harper Turner and J.H. Turner in the affluent neighborhood that developed as a result of the burgeoning timber industry. The neighborhood, founded in 1884, was also home to several of the city's founders and early economic developers.


Whitehall (Hardy Estate)
607 Third Street South
Columbus, MS 39701

Whitehall, also referred to as the Hardy Estate, is a stately mansion built in 1843 by James Walton Harris in the Greek Revival style. This antebellum house has paneled columns with hardwood balusters bordering the porch. Inside is beautiful woodwork and a collection of eighteenth- and nineteenth-century antiques. Whitehall is listed in the National Register of Historic Places.


William Johnson House
210 State Street
Natchez MS 39120

Known as the "Barber of Natchez," William Johnson (1809–1851) was a freed Black man who built his home in Natchez in 1840. Emancipated at age eleven by the white man believed to be his father, Johnson sought equal opportunities during a difficult time in America's history. As his assets grew, he and his family lived in the upstairs section of their house and rented the main floor to merchants. For sixteen years, he meticulously kept a diary comprising fourteen leather-bound volumes, now part of the museum's collection. Johnson was killed in a dispute over land boundaries. Visitors can view the family's living quarters to see what life was like for the Johnsons in the mid-1800s. Also on exhibit are artifacts and other memorabilia. The Ellicott Hill Preservation Society purchased the house in 1976 and later donated it to the City of Natchez. The National Park Service accepted the house as a donation from the city and opened it as a museum in 2005.

# MUSEUMS LISTED BY CITY AND MAP

**Aberdeen**
John Holliday House also known as Holliday Haven
The Magnolias

**Amory**
The City of Amory Regional Museum

**Baldwyn**
Brice's Cross Roads National Battlefield - Crossroads Visitors and Mississippi
   Final Stands Interpretive Center

**Bay St. Louis**
Bay St. Louis Historic L&N Train Depot (Alice Moseley Folk Art Museum
   and Bay St. Louis Mardi Gras Museum)
Beauvoir, the Jefferson Davis Home and Presidential Library
Kate Lobrano House

**Belzoni**
Catfish Museum and Welcome Center
Ethel Wright Mohamed Stitchery Museum
Jaketown Museum
Rev. George Lee Museum of African American History and Heritage and
   Fannie Lou Hamer Civil Rights Museum

## Biloxi
Maritime & Seafood Industry Museum
Ohr-O'Keefe Museum of Art
Pleasant Reed House
West End Fire Company No. 3

## Booneville
Rails and Trails Museum

## Brandon
Rankin County Historical Museum

## Brookhaven
Lincoln County Historical & Genealogical Society

## Bruce
Bruce Forestry Museum

## Camp Shelby
Mississippi Armed Forces Museum

## Canton
Canton Depot Museum
Canton History Museum
Canton (Film) Movie Museum
Canton Multi-Cultural Museum
Old Madison County Jail

## Carrollton
Mississippi John Hurt Museum
Merrill Museum

## Centreville
Camp Van Dorn World War II Museum

## Clarksdale
Aaron Cotton Company Museum
Carnegie Public Library Archeology Collection
Delta Blues Museum

Tennessee Williams Rectory Museum
WROX Museum

## Cleveland
Charles W. Capps Archives and Museum
Fielding L. Wright Art Center / Holcombe-Norwood Hall
GRAMMY Museum Mississippi
Martin and Sue King Railroad Heritage Museum

## Clinton
Samuel Marshall Gore Art Gallery

## Collins
Mitchell Farms

## Columbia
Marion County Museum

## Columbus
American Indian Artifacts Museum
Columbus War Museum
Eugenia Summers Gallery and MUW Fine Art Gallery
R.E. Hunt Museum and Cultural Center
Stephen D. Lee Home & Museum and Florence McLeod Hazard Museum
Temple Heights Mansion
Tennessee Williams House & Welcome Center Museum
Whitehall (Hardy Estate)

## Corinth
Black History Museum of Corinth
Borroum's Drug Store and Soda Fountain
Corinth Contraband Camp
Corinth Coca-Cola Museum
Corinth Civil War Interpretive Center
Crossroads Museum and the Historic Corinth Depot
Dream Riderz Classic Cars & Collectibles
Kossuth Museum
Lake Hill Motors Museum

**Crystal Springs**
Robert Johnson Museum

**DeKalb**
Kemper County Historical Museum

**Ellisville**
Amos Deason Home

**Flora**
Mississippi Petrified Forest

**French Camp**
French Camp Historic Area

**Friars Point**
North Delta Museum at Friars Point

**Glendora**
Emmett Till Historic Intrepid Center – E.T.H.I.C. Museum

**Greenville**
1927 Flood Museum
Century of History Museum at the Hebrew Union Temple
Delta Children's Museum
Greenville Air Force Base Museum
Greenville Blues History Museum and Gallery
Old Number 1 Firehouse Museum
River Road Queen Welcome Center and Museum of the Delta
Winterville Mounds and Museum

**Greenwood**
Back in the Day Museum
Greenwood Blues Heritage Museum and Gallery
Museum of the Mississippi Delta

**Grenada**
Grenada Lake Museum
Historical Museum / Coca-Cola Display

## Gulfport
Institute for Marine Mammal Studies
Lynn Meadows Discovery Center
TrainTastic™ Museum

## Hattiesburg
African American Military Museum
de Grummond Children's Literature Collection
Hattiesburg Historical Society Museum
Lucile Parker Gallery
Sarah Gillespie Museum of Art
Turner House Museum
USM Museum of Art

## Hazlehurst
Hazlehurst Depot Museum

## Hernando
DeSoto County Museum

## Holly Springs
Antebellum Davis House, Strawberry Plains Audubon Center
Ida B. Wells Barnett Museum
Kate Freeman Clark Art Gallery
Marshall County Historical Museum
Rust College, Roy Wilkins Collection at the Leontyne Price Library
Yellow Fever Martyrs Church & Museum

## Horn Lake
American Contract Bridge League Museum and Bridge Hall of Fame

## Houston
Chickasaw County Heritage Museum

## Indianola
B.B. King Museum & Delta Interpretive Center

## Iuka
Apron Museum
Old Tishomingo County Courthouse and Museum

## Jackson
Eudora Welty House
Governor's Mansion
International Museum of Muslim Cultures
Jackson Fire Museum
Manship House Museum
Medgar and Myrlie Evers Home National Monument
Mississippi Agriculture and Forestry Museum
Mississippi Children's Museum
Mississippi Museum of Art
Mississippi Museum of Natural Science
Mississippi Music Experience at the Iron Horse Grill
Mississippi Sports Hall of Fame and Museum
Mississippi State Hospital Museum
Municipal Art Gallery of Jackson
Oaks House Museum
Old Capitol Museum
Smith Robertson Museum and Cultural Center
Two Mississippi Museums (Museum of Mississippi History and Mississippi
    Civil Rights Museum)
War Memorial Building

## Kosciusko
Kosciusko Museum and Visitors Center

## Laurel
Landrum's Country Homestead and Village
Lauren Rogers Museum of Art
Veterans Memorial Museum

## Leakesville
Greene County Museum & Historical Society

## Leland
Highway 61 Blues Museum
Jim Henson Delta Boyhood Museum (The Birthplace of Kermit the Frog)
Mississippi Wildlife Heritage Museum

**Louisville**
American Heritage "Big Red" Fire Museum

**Macon**
Noxubee County Historical Society Museum

**McComb**
The Black History Gallery

**Meridian**
Jimmie Rodgers Museum
Key Brothers Aviation Museum, Meridian Regional Airport
Lauderdale County Department of Archives and History
Meridian Museum of Art
Meridian Railroad Museum
Merrehope
Mississippi Arts + Entertainment Experience (The Max)
Mississippi Children's Museum
Mississippi Industrial Heritage Museum (Soulé Steam Feed Works)

**Monticello**
A.H. Longino House
Lawrence County Regional History Museum

**Mound Bayou**
Mound Bayou Museum of African American Culture and History

**Natchez**
Grand Village of the Natchez Indians
Longwood
Magnolia Hall
Melrose Mansion
Mount Locust
Museum of Jewish Experience
Natchez Museum of African American History and Culture
Rosalie Mansion and Gardens
Stanton Hall
William Johnson House

## New Albany
Union County Historical Society and Heritage Museum

## Ocean Springs
G.I. Museum
William M. Colmer Visitor Center, Gulf Islands National Seashore, Mississippi District
Marine Education Center
Walter Anderson Museum of Art

## Oxford
Burns-Belfry Museum & Multicultural Center
L.Q.C. Lamar House
Mary Buie Museum
Rowan Oak
University of Mississippi Museum

## Pascagoula
LaPointe-Krebs House and Museum (Old Spanish Fort)

## Pearlington
NASA John C. Stennis Space Center, INFINITY Science Center

## Philadelphia
Chahta Immi Cultural Center
Marty Stuart's Congress of Country Music
Philadelphia–Neshoba County Historical Society

## Picayune
Carver Culture Museum
Crosby Arboretum
Hilda Hoffman Memorial Archive Inc.
Teddy Bear Museum

## Piney Woods
Laurence C. Jones Museum

## Pontotoc
Town Square Post Office and Museum

**Poplarville**
Pearl River Community College Museum

**Port Gibson**
Grand Gulf Military Monument Park

**Raymond**
Marie Hull Gallery

**Ridgeland**
Craftsmen's Guild of Mississippi, William Waller Crafts Center

**Ripley**
Tippah County Historical Museum

**Robinsonville**
Tunica RiverPark Museum

**Sandy Hook**
John Ford Home

**Sardis**
Heflin House Museum

**Senatobia**
Tate County Heritage Museum

**Starkville**
Charles H. Templeton, Sr. Music Museum
Cobb Archaeology Museum/Cobb Institute of Archaeology
Cullis & Gladys Wade Clock Museum
Dunn-Seiler Geology Museum
Frank and Virginia Williams Collection of Lincolniana Gallery
John Grisham Room
Mississippi Entomological Museum
Oktibbeha County Heritage Museum
Ulysses S. Grant Presidential Library Museum

**Sturgis**
(Craig and Elaine Vechnorik's) Bench Mark Works LLC Motorcycle Museum

**Taylorsville**
Watkins Museum

**Tunica**
Gateway to the Blues Museum and Visitors Center
Tunica Museum

**Tupelo**
Elvis Presley Birthplace
(Elvis) Presley Heights Museum
Gumtree Museum of Art
HealthWorks! A Children's Museum
Oren Dunn City Museum
Tupelo Veterans Museum

**Utica**
Utica Institute Museum

**Vicksburg**
Biedenharn Coca-Cola Museum
Catfish Row Museum
Jacqueline House African American Museum
Jesse Brent Lower Mississippi River Museum
McRaven House
Old Court House Museum
Old Depot Museum
Pemberton's Headquarters
USS Cairo Gunboat and Museum
Vicksburg Battlefield Museum
Vicksburg Civil War Museum
Vicksburg National Military Park, Visitors Center / Museum

**Water Valley**
Casey Jones Railroad Museum

**Waveland**
Waveland's Ground Zero Hurricane Museum

**West Point**
Howlin' Wolf Museum
Mann-East-Friday House Museum
Sam Wilhite Transportation Museum

**Whitfield**
Mississippi State Hospital Museum

**Woodville**
African American Museum
Rosemont Plantation
Wilkinson County Museum

**Yazoo City**
Oakes African American Cultural Center
Sam B. Olden Yazoo Historic Society Museum

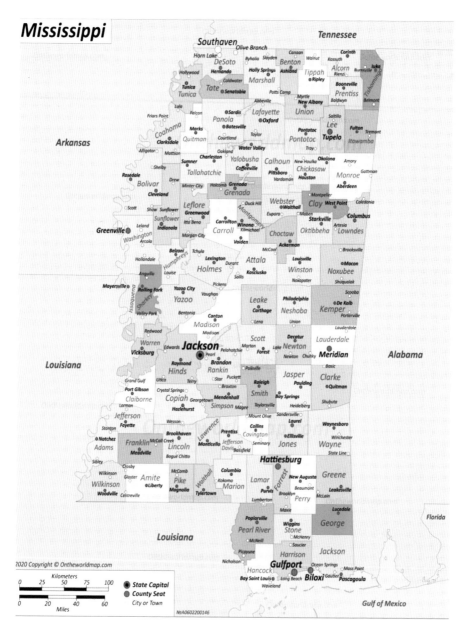

County and city map of Mississippi. *On the World Map.com. info@ontheworldmap.com.*

# ABOUT THE AUTHORS

DIANE WILLIAMS has over sixteen years of art administration to her credit, along with a background as a professional storyteller. RICHELLE PUTNAM holds an MA in writing and is a successful freelance writer and editor. Both writers have multiple award-winning books to their credit.